QUÉBEC

☑ S0-DLD-450

APA PUBLICATIONS
Part of the Langenscheidt Publishing Group

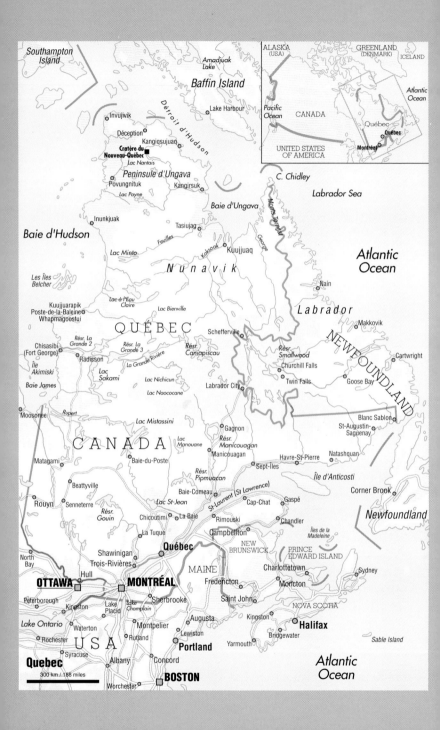

Southampton Island

Amadjuak Lake

Baffin Island

Invujivik

Lake Harbour

Détroit d'Hudson

Déception

Kangiqsujuaq

Cratère du
Nouveau-Québec

Lac Nantais

C. Chidley

Labrador Sea

Peninsule d'Ungava

Povungnituk

Kangirsuk

Baie d'Ungava

Lac Payne

Inunkjuak

Tasiujaq

Kuujjuaq

Baie d'Hudson

Lac Minto

Feuilles

Koksoak

George

Nunavik

Atlantic Ocean

Les Îles Belcher

Lac à l'Eau Claire

Lac Bienville

Labrador

Naín

Kuujjuarapik
Poste-de-la-Baleine
Whapmagoostui

QUÉBEC

Scheffervile

Makkovik

NEWFOUNDLAND

Cartwright

Chisasibi
(Fort George)

Résr. La Grande 2

Résr. La Grande 3

Résr. Caniapiscau

Résr. Smallwood

Radisson

La Grande Rivière

Churchill Falls

Île Akimiski

Lac Sakami

Lac Nichicun

Twin Falls

Goose Bay

Baie James

Lac Naococane

Labrador City

Moosonee

Rupert

Lac Mistassini

Gagnon

Blanc Sablon
St-Augustin-Saguenay

Newfoundland

CANADA

Lac Manouane

Résr. Manicouagan

Natashquan

Matagami

Baie-du-Poste

Manicouagan

Havre-St-Pierre

Corner Brook

Beattyville

Résr. Pipmuacan

Sept-Îles

Île d'Anticosti

Rouyn

Senneterre

Résr. Gouin

Baie-Comeau

St-Laurent (St Lawrence)

Cap-Chat

Gaspé

Chicoutimi

La Baie

Lac St-Jean

Rimouski

Chandler

La Tuque

Campbellton

Îles de la Madeleine

Shawinigan

Québec

NEW BRUNSWICK

PRINCE EDWARD ISLAND

North Bay

Trois-Rivières

Hull

MONTRÉAL

MAINE

Charlottetown

Sydney

OTTAWA

Fredericton

Moncton

Peterborough

Kingston

Lake Placid

Lac Champlain

Sherbrooke

Saint John

NOVA SCOTIA

Lake Ontario

Waterton

Montpelier

Augusta

Kingston

Halifax

Rochester

Syracuse

Rutland

Lewiston

Bridgewater

Yarmouth

Sable Island

USA

Albany

Concord

Portland

Quebec

300 km / 188 miles

Worchester

BOSTON

Atlantic Ocean

ALASKA (USA)

GREENLAND (DENMARK)

ICELAND

Pacific Ocean

CANADA

Atlantic Ocean

Québec

Québec

UNITED STATES OF AMERICA

Montréal

Welcome!

This guidebook combines the interests and enthusiasms of two of the world's best-known information providers: Insight Guides, who have set the standard for visual travel guides since 1970, and Discovery Channel, the world's premier source of nonfiction television programming. It aims to bring you the best of Québec and its surroundings in tailor-made itineraries devised by Insight's correspondent, Alice Klement.

Québec is a big province, encompassing fast-changing Montréal, historic Québec City, a varied coastline, and the wilderness of Nunavik. Klement helps travelers make sense of this large slice of Canada in 16 carefully crafted itineraries based on seven key areas – Québec City, Montréal, the Laurentians, the Eastern Townships, Charlevoix, the Gaspé Peninsula and Nunavik. Her city-based tours are geared for walking and, in the case of Montréal, hopping on the Metro, while the regional itineraries require a car. Favorite restaurants and accommodation en route are also recommended.

 Alice Klement moved to Québec from the US to work as a researcher for film and television. Enchanted by French-flavored Montréal, she wrote *Insight Pocket Guide: Montréal*. She then set out to learn more about the rest of Québec – from Gaspé fishermen to farmers in the Eastern Townships and ski buffs in the Laurentians. She hopes that this guide has something for everyone, whether they want to sample *haute cuisine* or go whale-watching off Tadoussac.

Pages 2/3:
Québec, first
city on the
St Lawrence

Pages 10/11: Faces in the countryside

HISTORY & CULTURE

In the late 1980s, the builders of Québec City's innovative Musée de la Civilisation unearthed a boat that had been buried for more than 200 years. In a province where history is highly cherished but often revised, this *barque* is more evocative than provocative, for it was just such anonymous craft that opened Québec to exploration and exploitation.

In 1534, French navigator Jacques Cartier sailed into a Gaspésian cove and planted a cross on a rocky, windswept plateau. Today, such markers flourish throughout Québec. Indeed, sleek stelae anchor the spot that Cartier touched – a modern monument to an old one. In 1608, fellow explorer Samuel de Champlain founded a colony at *Kebec*. By 1642, settlers were arriving at the Iroquois homeland of Hochelaga, which, a century earlier, Cartier had renamed *Mont Réal*.

Though explorers conveniently proclaimed this land *Terra Nullus* – empty of people – this was not quite the case. European *voyageurs* befriended natives, adopting their canoes and snowshoes to survive in the harsh environment. Indeed, only a peace treaty with the Iroquois in 1701 assured New France's survival. (Back then, Amerindians had enough power to debunk claims that only the French are pure

Samuel de Champlain

Québecers. Today, with their numbers reduced to 55,000, they are now striving to regain some of that power.)

When Québec City became the administrative capital of New France in 1663, colonial power was finally focused. Until then, fur companies responsible for settling land had been concerned with consolidating profits, not colonization. The *coureurs des bois* – independent heroes of myth, but hard-nosed fur company men in reality – tracked beavers to cater for what rapidly became a European fashion frenzy. As demand for fur boosted Montréal and Québec City as trading posts and ports of entry, so immigrants arrived, although not very willingly. In 150 years of French rule, all but an estimated 500 of 10,000 settlers came as indentured servants, soldiers, or convicts.

Along the River

In the years after 1663, Europeans – the French along the river banks and on the plains, the English on the seaboard – overwhelmed both natives and nature. Unlike trappers, colonists preferred European institutions to Indian ways. So when French farmers clustered in the St Lawrence valley, Amerindians too close to European civilization lost their own. In short order, the newcomers took the river and its fish; the animals and their fur; the forests and their timber; the fields with their wheat and ore.

From the start, the St Lawrence was Québec's *rue principale*, and boats like the museum's *barque* ferried goods and news to farmers on narrow *rangs* along its shores. Even now, hulls beached in the Gaspé or dry-docked in Charlevoix testify to a grand past. Québec City earned international accolades for boat building; Montréal became the world's largest inland port, with a flow of timber, wheat, fish, pulp and paper, and now tourists.

Despite revisionist fondness for *la vie d'antan* (the good old days), early colonial life was rigid. As in France, landowners and clergy – often the same *seigneurs* – controlled the people from cradle to grave. By the mid-1700s, clerics had cornered much of the land, Jesuits in Québec City and and Sulpicians in Montréal. Elsewhere, parish priests held sway, their authority lasting until the mid-20th century. Zealous laity also helped, with prominent women founding hospitals and religious communities. Gradually, other women arrived to bolster the colony's population. Those *filles du roi*, foremothers of 95 percent of Québec's francophones, are now the subject of debate: were they French heroines, or Huguenot whores?

Early map of Québec City

As New France expanded across half a continent in the late 1600s, Old World rivals battled for supremacy in the New. France fortified its provincial cities to block invaders. But the British controlled the seas and sent a navy to besiege Québec City in 1759, its troops victorious in a surprise skirmish on the Plains of Abraham. Within a year, the French surrendered at Montréal, ceding Québec in the 1763 Treaty of Paris.

The conquest revisited

Predictably, points of view differ widely over this clash of empires. Anglophones tout the start of Canada's bicultural society. Francophones bemoan a catastrophe. Despite that gap, Québec City now offers perhaps the only monument in the world to honor victor and vanquished of the same battle: Britain's General Wolfe and France's Marquis de Montcalm, both killed in combat. And nearby, today's

centre d'interprétation in Battlefields Park is so balanced, so even-handed, so politically correct that who won may now be in doubt. Yet the province's motto, *Je me souviens* (I remember), etched on the *Assemblée* doorway and repeated on the province's license plates, still rallies defenders of Québec's French language and culture, begging the question: is reconciliation possible?

Oddly, cultural defense, and *Québécois* separatism, may have started with the British. In 1774, to thwart the power of American rev-

Nineteenth-century image of French settlers

olutionaries, the new rulers passed the Québec Act, guaranteeing French customs and religion. The Americans retreated from Québec and some 70,000 British Loyalists 'invaded,' settling the Eastern Townships and the Gaspé Peninsula.

Peace brought industrial development, improved communications and prosperity in its wake. In 1809, steamboats linked Montréal and Québec City; by 1891, trains, telegraphs and telephones strengthened the links between these two cities. In the 1820s, Québec harnessed water in flour, saw, and carding mills – all precursors of the grand-scale hydroelectric plants now transforming the north of the province. Public subsidies financed growth, creating the Lachine Canal in 1820, the Victoria Bridge in 1859. Once the province established a civil code and dismantled archaic seigneurialism, modern Québec started to emerge.

Late-19th-century Québec

Strikes, riots, even refusals to take communion, ensued. In 1837, French Canadian *patriotes* demanded recognition in a rebellion led by Louis-Joseph Papineau. A decade later, angry over *patriote* pardons, Tories sacked parliament, costing Montreal its status as the country's capital. In 1867, Québec joined the new Confederation of Canada. But anti-federalism still flourished. The conservative Société St Jean Baptiste, a fraternal organization touting anti-imperialism, claimed the maple leaf from the *patriote* flag – a full century before Canada did. (Each 24 June, on Québec's *fête nationale*, *Québécois* brandish *fleur-de-lis*, borrowed from the French army and sewn into the provincial flag in 1950.) Yet not all Québec political leaders were firebrands. Wilfrid Laurier, Canada's first francophone prime minister, won on a platform of 'sunny ways' – faith in anglophone goodwill.

Economic boomlets

Meanwhile, the province's economy took new shape. After the conquest, Scots and other anglophone immigrants reorganized the fur trade and expanded into other industries, in particular mining and forestry. Industrialists clustered in Montréal's Golden Square Mile, amassing fortunes and building opulent mansions. But anglophone capitalism was uneven, bypassing rural francophone farmers who considered business *l'affaire d'anglais*.

Migrations – from country to city and back; from province and abroad and back – soon convulsed Québec. In 1850, when 80 percent of Québecers lived in rural areas, only the farmers on the Montréal plain and near Québec City thrived. As poverty crippled more remote regions, thousands fled to city jobs, to work side by side with foreign immigrants. To counter this, priests glorified pastoral family life and called for a *revanche des berceaux* (revenge of the cradle) to preserve French culture. (Once tallying one of the highest Western birthrates, Québec now has one of the lowest, cut one-third between 1960 and 1970. Clerics once offered to educate the 26th child in a family. Now the province subsidizes births.)

Between 1840 and 1930, more than 900,000 French Canadians left Québec, many heading to work in the US. To stem the exodus, po-

Basilique Ste-Anne de Beaupré

litical and religious leaders promoted free land in isolated regions, down-playing such vital drawbacks as poor soil. Desperate pioneers headed to the Laurentians and the Gaspé, but 'colonization' failed. It would be wealthy socialites who championed Charlevoix, ski buffs who brought prosperity to the Laurentians.

Québec, especially Montréal, became a magnet for poor immigrants from Europe, notably Eastern European Jews, Greeks, Italians and Portuguese. By 1930, two decades of immigration had doubled the city's population to a million. The new religions and radical ideas introduced by these newcomers riled conservatives, with the clergy railing against such 'isms' as materialism, communism, unionism. By the 1930s, cleric intellectual Lionel Groulx touted 'Québec First' fervently enough to re-kindle *Québécois* nationalism. As church power soared, so did such symbols as the Oratoire St-Joseph in Montréal and the Basilique Ste-Anne-de-Beaupré outside Québec City. The steeples stayed but influence ebbed a few years later, when poor Québecers discovered that even church charity could not cope with the Depression.

While clerics preached obedience to authority, agitators preached disobedience – of conscription laws in World War I and, later, World War II. Reluctant to join a military infused with Britain's language and traditions, Québec protestors blasted imperialism as they battled the draft.

During the days of the *Grande noirceur* –the great darkness – in the 1940s and 1950s, conservative ideology and church power marked Québec society. Québec premier Maurice Duplessis opened agricultural schools and improved rural roads, but fought the formation of unions and the march of industrialization.

Immigrants arrive

For decades, intellectuals, labor progressives, political reformers, and moderate Catholics worked for change, battling Duplessis's long rule. In the 1960s, they stirred social forces into political realities, a *révolution tranquille* (quiet revolution) replacing clergy with civil servants, church with state. Within a few years, progressives secularized schools, nationalized industries, universalized health care, and bolstered francophone entrepreneurs with *caisse populaire* funds. Artists were not slow to encourage cultural changes. In search of *l'identité Québécois,* playwright Michel Tremblay used distinctive tones of Montréal's street slang *joual.* Balladeer Félix Leclerc touted distinct *Québécois* qualities. Singers Robert Charlebois and Diane Dufresne added francophone flavor to rock 'n' roll. In a bid for international recognition, Montréal hosted a World Expo in 1967 and the Summer Olympics in 1976. Both triggered development in downtown Montréal. The fair added glory; the sports added debt.

(Hydro-development also opened the north, after Inuit and Amerindians signed the 1975 James Bay Agreement on land claims.)

Peaceful exhortations – France's President Charles de Gaulle shouting '*Vive le Québec Libre*' – turned violent in 1970 when Front de Libération du Québec terrorists set off more than 200 bombs. In the face of FLQ kidnappings and murder, federalist Prime Minister Pierre Trudeau dispatched the army to Montréal. Debate still lingers over

Hydro-electric plants blossomed

what francophones call *événements* (events) and anglophones see as the 'October crisis.' (Twenty years later, in an equally rare display of Canadian violence, Mohawks confronted the Sureté du Québec over disputed land, and federal troops again intervened. The Mohawks sported Warrior T-shirts, not headdresses.)

In Québec, where nationalism allies with the French language, recent decades have brought elections, by-elections, referendums, constitutional conventions, anglophone anguish and francophone backlash. Over 20 years the province passed language laws, some indecipherable, others indigestible. In 1977, after the separatist Parti Québécois (PQ) won a surprise victory at provincial polls, Québec ignored Canada's official bilingualism and promoted French only. (More recent bills have allowed English on commercial signs, provided French is dominant.) With these restrictions on the use of English, name changes swept the province. Knowlton was resurrected as *Lac-Brome*, the Eastern Townships reconstituted first as *L'Estrie*, and now as *Cantons-de-L'Est.* Language riots flared in Montréal suburbs, and immigrants and anglophones fled as *fleur-de-lis* flew. Yet in 1980, a majority of Québecers rejected 'sovereignty

Canadian premier Trudeau

association' in a referendum. The vote was a blow to René Lévesque, PQ leader, popular Québec premier and opponent of charismatic bi-lingual Prime Minister Pierre Trudeau, who favored co-operation over separation.

In 1987, at Meech Lake, backers of Canada's constitution promised Québec status as a 'distinct society' in exchange for its signature. Then, when two of the provincial parliaments raised objections, Québec refused to sign. The Meech Lake Agreement collapsed in 1990, and the Charlottestown Accord followed suit in 1992.

Was this a stalemate? In 1993, the separatist Bloc Québécois became Canada's opposition party, and in 1994 voters in Québec elected the Parti Québécois, a party dedicated to separating from Canada, led by Jacques Parizeau. The failure of his promised 1995 referendum saw Lucien Bouchard switching from federal to provincial politics, to take over the PQ's reins. His election promise in 1998 to create "winning conditions" for sovereignty ensured another electoral win by the PQ. Since then, however, Bouchard has had to focus on playing down Québec's deficit.

Sporting the fleur-de-lis

Such turmoil already challenges revisionist historians. To honor the 350th anniversary of Montréal's founding, archeologists sifted through centuries of dirt to find *objets* to encase in glass at Pointe à Callière, where settlers first landed. Unlike in Québec City, they found no unique *barque*. Nevertheless, the city honored the past. In 1994 officials erected a modern granite monument, *Memoire Ardente*, in its old plaza. Its bilingual explanation recollects city sites and sounds.

But what does it mean? Québec's two museums of civilization, one opened by the PQ in Québec City and one by the federal government in Hull, often offer conflicting interpretations. You'll discover there, as everywhere in the province, that not everything is resolved, and that *mémoires* never die.

Historical Highlights

1000 Amerindians populate the south, Inuit the north.

1535 Jacques Cartier is the first European to arrive at Amerindian homeland at Hochelaga, near present-day Montréal.

1608 Samuel Champlain founds Québec City.

1642 Colonists settle Montréal.

1663 New France is placed under royal jurisdiction.

1670 At James Bay, the Hudson's Bay Company draws Amerindians into fur trade.

1701 Peace treaty between French and Iroquois.

1759 Québec City capitulates to British forces after Plains of Abraham skirmish. Montréal surrenders a year later.

1763 France signs Treaty of Paris, which relinquishes New France to England.

1764 The Québec *Gazette*, North America's oldest newspaper, still publishing as *The Chronicle Telegraph*, is founded in Québec City.

1774 Act of Québec protects French civil law and Catholic religion.

1775 Americans besiege Québec City and enter Montréal.

1791 Constitution divides Canada, with Québec City as capital of French-speaking Lower Canada.

1821 McGill University is founded in Montréal.

1824 Lachine Canal opens.

1829 *Basilique Notre-Dame*, once the largest church in North America, opens in Montréal.

1837 *Les Patriotes* rebellion fails.

1841 The Act of Union unites Upper and Lower Canada into a single jurisdiction.

1844 Montréal serves briefly as capital of United Canada.

1852 Québec City's Université Laval is founded as North America's first French-language Catholic university.

1859 Victoria Bridge spans St Lawrence River.

1860 Musée des beaux arts opens in Montreal.

1867 Québec joins new Dominion of Canada.

1886 Canada's first transcontinental train leaves Montréal.

1917 World's longest cantilevered bridge holds at Québec City

1924 Construction of St Joseph's Oratory begins.

1940 Women win provincial vote.

1959 St Lawrence Seaway opens.

1968 Québec's Pierre Trudeau becomes Canada's prime minister. Separatist Parti Québécois founded.

1962 Development of Montréal's underground city and metro.

1967 Montréal hosts Expo '67.

1970 Front de Libération du Québec terrorism draws federal troops.

1975 James Bay agreement with Amerindians and Inuit opens hydroelectric development in north.

1976 Montréal hosts Summer Olympics. René Lévesque is elected Québec premier.

1977 Charter of French Language is passed.

1980 Sovereignty association fails.

1983 Québec enacts charter of rights and freedoms.

1985 UNESCO names Québec City as 'world heritage treasure.'

1990 Mohawks and police confrontation at Oka.

1990 Meech Lake accord collapses.

1993 Québecer Jean Chrétien is elected Canada's prime minister.

1994 Premier-elect Parizeau promises referendum on independence.

1995 October 30. Referendum on Québec sovereignty results in vote of 50.6 percent No, to 49.5 percent Yes.

1995 November. Jacques Parizeau resigns as Québec Premier.

1996 January Parti Québécois leader Lucien Bouchard becomes Québec Premier.

1998 Parti Québécois wins another election under Bouchard.

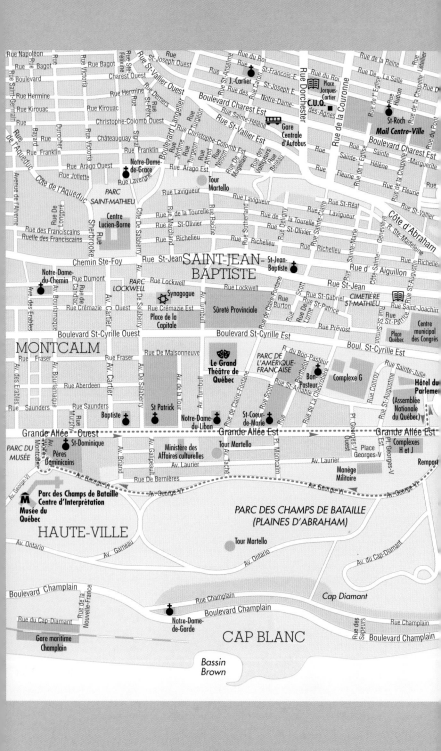

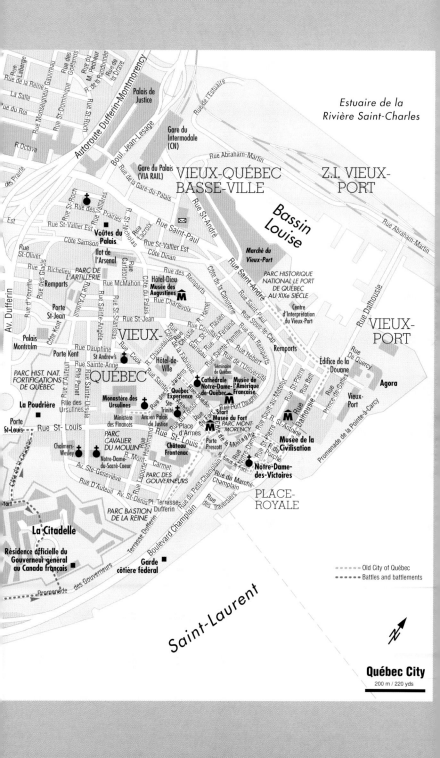

Québec City

200 m / 220 yds

Québec City

Comparisons are often made between Québec City and Montréal. While the latter is more sophisticated, the former is more historically intact, and its residents claim that it is the province's spiritual heart – although they may be biased, of course.

Proud of its heritage

Founded in 1608, the city looks its age: not a 'heritage center,' despite UNESCO's recognition that the continent's largest collection of 17th- and 18th-century buildings is 'a world heritage treasure,' but an appealingly real, work-a-day town.

If you are traveling to Québec City from Montréal (a distance of 253km/158 miles), follow Highway 40 northeast. Signs saying 'Québec' mean Québec City. Ideas on where to stay are contained in the *Practical Information* section of this guide.

The following three tours concentrate on the highlights of Québec City. They explore the **Basse-Ville** (Lower Town) and the **Haute-Ville** (Upper Town), inside the ancient fortifications, plus the 'newer' city outside the walls, and suggest a trip outside the city to the Ile d'Orléans. The labyrinth of streets and alleys in the old city is best explored on foot, but if you really need wheels, rent a bicycle, as some streets are pedestrian precincts and parking is almost impossible.

1. The old city of Québec

This day tour takes in the sacred and the secular: both of Québec's cathedrals, the historic Notre-Dame-des-Victoires, the Musée de la civilisation, and the Musée de l'Amérique française, a boardwalk stroll and a seafood lunch. See map on pages 18/19.

To start your tour, head to Lower Town (Basse-Ville) via Rue du Fort or Côte de la Montagne. The Lower Town is just a boat's row from the St Lawrence river which brought Québec its prosperity and growth. For a unique historical overview of the province, explore the **Musée de la civilisation** (late June to early September: daily 10am–7pm; September to June: Tuesday to Sunday 10am–5pm), 85 rue Dalhousie, tel: 418 643-2158. Its second-floor exhibit on **Mémoires** explores the past and makes sense of the present in a way

that appeals to both intellect and emotions. **La Barque**, on the first floor, a recovered and restored 18th-century boat, is another popular item. Other exhibits offer insight, even whimsy – the history of cosmetics, the saga of stripes. This museum is hands-on, so feel free to turn knobs and push buttons. The average visit lasts four hours, time well spent. On busy summer days, attendance has topped 10,000. If it is very crowded, consider a cursory visit and a possible return off-hours.

The building itself is astounding. Architect Moshe Safdie's modern design blends an 18th-century warehouse with copper, stone, and glass-campanile to match the neighborhood's mansard roofs, stone parapets, and steeples. Even the entryway offers drama. Look for the mammoth sculpture *La Débâcle* that captures the crackle of spring's splintering ice.

Afterwards, try **le Café du Monde**, 57 rue Dalhousie, tel: 418 692-4455, for breakfast (Saturdays and Sundays only) or bistro specialties such as garlic snails. Or walk up rue Dalhousie to **Marché du Vieux-Port** at 160 quai St-André to haggle over farm-fresh fruit and flowers in the port-side market. Then head south on rue Dalhousie to **Place-Royale**, where, in 1608, Samuel de Champlain established a fort and trading post called the Habitation, on the flats between cliffs and river. Only later did the struggling port become Kebec, the Algonquin word for 'the place where the river narrows.' Little more than a staging point for expeditions, the town drew settlers only when its defenses improved later in the 17th century.

Commercial activity centered in the Lower Town – with wharves, counting houses, and fur warehouses, it was a dock-side home to merchants and laborers. Its cobblestoned commercial heart, Place-Royale, still draws summer-time street vendors and performers. Here also stands the **Eglise Notre-Dame-des-Victoires**, the city's most historic church (May 1 to October 15: daily 9.30am–4:30pm; October 16

Place-Royale

Château Frontenac

to May 1: daily 10am–4.30pm). Its frescoes detail British sieges in 1690 and 1711, both of which the town resisted.

Legend has it that the patroness of Paris, St Geneviève, promises prosperity to anyone who carries bread crumbs. So, each year, local women bake 100,000 loaves, which are left chunk by chunk in bowls beside the altar. Help yourself! At the opposite end of Place-Royale, the side of an old building at the corner of côté de la Montagne and rue Notre-Dame sports an immense and intriguing trompe-l'oeil fresco that depicts people and architecture in Québec City from the 1600s to today.

Rely on the plaza's bust of the Sun King Louis XIV as your landmark. Wander around **Le Quartier Petit-Champlain**, where lanes shoot off at unexpected angles. Along Petit-Champlain itself, just off the square, you'll absorb *Nouvelle France* style – thick stone walls, dormer windows, bright tin roofs, wooden doors and shutters. More than 50 shops run the gamut from A to Z: Artista Fabrica to Zazou jewelry. Lunch on *crêpes* or *soup de jour* at tiny restaurants and sidewalk cafés. Consider **Le Marie Clarisse** at 12 Petit-Champlain, tel: 418 692-0857. Housed in a 350-year-old stone building, this haven for seafood-lovers offers salmon from the Gaspé and striped bass from the St Lawrence. Indulge – you'll need energy for the climb that is to come.

Almost 100m (300ft) above, in the Upper Town (Haute-Ville), looms the cliff that French navigator Jacques Cartier named Cap Diamant when he wintered nearby in the 16th century. (It's a misnomer: he optimistically believed the quartz crystals on the beach were diamonds – hence 'as fake as Canadian diamonds.')

To get to the *cap* from Lower Town, you must move a century through history and climb **L'escalier Casse-Cou** (Breakneck Stairs) from rue Sous-le-Fort to côte de la Montagne. Or you could take the less strenuous route: the glass-enclosed **funicular** (all year long 7.30am–10.50pm in winter; 7.30am–midnight in summer) at 16 Petit-Champlain. Its station is Maison Louis Jolliet, the 1683 home of the Québecer who discovered the Mississippi River. The ride up,

Terrasse Duferin

hugging the cliff at a 45 degree angle, delivers extensive views of another world-class river, the St Lawrence – and all for a loonie, as the one-dollar coins are amusingly known locally.

Exit onto the boardwalk near **Château Frontenac**, a huge copper-roofed castle – the city's landmark silhouette and arguably Canada's best-known hotel (tel: 418 691-2166 for tours). An American architect, Bruce Price, designed this *château*-style building in 1893 on the site of the colonial headquarters of the 17th-century governor of New France, Compte de Frontenac. Notice the fortress features: turrets, crenels, and parapets. Stroll through the elaborate entrance hall and peek into the main dining room. Originally designed for the Canadian Pacific Railways, the hotel is a national icon, as familiar as the mounties out west.

Nearby, **Terrasse Dufferin**, a boardwalk that stretches 671m (2,200ft), offers choice views: Lévis across the river, Ile d'Orléans, the Laurentides. Plunk a quarter in the telescope. From here, you can appreciate the importance of Québec's port, 1,368km (855 miles) inland, but open year-round. In 1831, the *Royal William*, the first steamboat to cross the Atlantic, was built and launched here. For the perfect sit-down view, treat yourself to tea at Château Frontenac's **Café de la Terrasse** (daily 7am–11pm).

The Terrasse Dufferin is also the site of an impressive statue of Samuel de Champlain, who gazes from his pedestal across the city which he founded. Nearby is the UNESCO monument which commemorates the fact that the historic district of Québec is on that organization's World Heritage List.

Leaving the terrace behind, head towards **Place d'Armes**, a small square beside the Château Frontenac. This *place* was known as the *Place Grande* during the *ancien régime*, when it hosted military pomp and civic speeches, but its role was usurped when La Citadelle (see Itinerary 2) was built in the mid-19th century. Now it is an attractive public park.

During the mid-1600s, soldiers constructed thick granite and sandstone walls in the Upper Town to help protect New France's lucrative fur and timber trade from the British. Stretching 4.6km (3 miles), the walls enclose 130ha (323 acres) of land, including among its buildings the star-shaped citadel. In the 1870s, a preservation-minded governor general of Canada, Lord Dufferin, insisted that the walls be preserved – a rare piece of foresight in North America at the time.

On a pedestal: Champlain

Inside the cathedral

The monastic orders also built here: their religious power is evident in the stone statues and stained glass of the convents and monasteries that enliven Upper Town. Explore these religious buildings *en masse* – they are all clustered near the square (tel: 418 694-0665 for tours).

La Cathédrale Notre-Dame-de-Québec, 20 rue Baude (daily 7.30am–4pm; tours: May to October: Monday to Friday 9am–2.30pm; Saturday 9am–4.30pm; Sunday 12.30–4.30pm), is gloomy but great – once ruling a diocese that stretched as far south as New Orleans. **Chapelle des Ursulines**, at 12 rue Donnacona (May to September: Tuesday to Saturday 10am–12noon, 1–5pm; Sunday 1–5pm), offers a pulpit with a trumpet-toting angel.

Founded in 1663, **le Grande Séminaire** at 9 rue de l'université was the province's first museum (1806) and Canada's first university (1852). It recently re-invented itself as **Musée de l'Amérique française** (June 24 to September 6: daily 10am–5.30pm; September 7 to June 23: Tuesday to Sunday 10am–5pm). Here is francophone memorabilia, both worldly and religious. Among its treasures, look for an Egyptian mummy, *sans* wrap, which was brought home by an *abbé* who had been touring the Holy Land.

Across the plaza from Château Frontenac and also worth a look inside is the **Cathédrale Anglicane de la Sainte-Trinité** (May and June, daily 9am–6pm; July and August, daily 9am–8pm; September to mid-October, daily 10am–4pm; guided tours; otherwise services only; evensong 4.45pm). This is the oldest Anglican cathedral outside the British Isles, built in 1793, and said to be modeled on St Martin-in-the-Fields in London.

Within a two-block radius, you can also discover visual pyrotechnics illuminating Québec's history. Running daily, there are almost non-stop presentations, which alternate French and English versions. You might end up more dazed than dazzled. Choose between:

• **Québec Expérience**, a 3D, multi-media holo-video (mid-May to mid-October: daily, 10am–10pm; October to May: Sunday to Thursday 10am–5pm; Friday and Saturday 10am–10pm), at 8 rue du Trésor.

• **Musée du Fort**, a room-size diorama replaying famous colonial battles (summer: daily 10am–7pm; times vary off-season), 10 rue Ste-Anne.

• **Rue du Trésor**, for a romp through the city's secular side. Prices at this open-air art gallery, off Place d'Armes, dip at day's and season's end.

If you want to shop or browse, consider going up and back along **rue St-Jean**, where big-name clothiers mix with small-name souvenir

Outside Aux Anciens Canadiens

shops. It's not for sale, but don't miss the scale model of Québec, circa 1806–8, at the reception center in **Parc de l'Artillerie** (May 8 to October 31, 10am–5pm; rest of the year, upon reservation; tel: 418 648-4205), 2 rue d'Auteil, near Porte St-Jean.

Next you could head along **rue St-Louis**, filled with tacky souvenir shops and tantalizing restaurants. Reserve early for dinner at **Aux Anciens Canadiens** at 34 rue St-Louis, tel: 418 692-1627. Its waitresses look authentic in old-time ruffles. Its food – caribou, goose, hare, duckling – *is* authentic. You're now within a short stroll of **Porte St-Louis**, the most photographed of the city's four gates. Pass through to **Grande Allée**, from old-old city to new-old city.

2. Battles and battlements

Today's tour begins with a visit to La Citadelle and takes in a visit to parliament en route to the Parc des Champs-de-Bataille and its museum, before lunch on historic Grande Allée. After lunch, take it easy with a calèche ride through the old city or a ferry trip from Lévis Dock.

For three centuries, Québec City, defender of northeast North America, was defined by fortifications. Oddly, construction got underway on its biggest, boldest bulwark – **la Citadelle** – in 1834, long after the city was last besieged, by American revolutionaries, in 1775. But who was to know that it would not one day be needed to defend the city?

To explore this military might, arrive early at the huge, star-shaped fortress at côte de la Citadelle. Home to the Canadian Armed Forces' Royal 22nd Regiment, the hilltop fort is partially open to the public, and there are

Changing the guard at la Citadelle

guided tours (summer: daily 9am–6pm, winter: times vary, tel: 418 694-2815). Enter through the Durnford Gate, named after Lieutenant-Colonel Elias Durnford, who supervised the construction of the fortress. A former powder magazine and military prison display firearms and uniforms, circa 1600 to the present. But the excitement starts with the changing of the guard at 10am every rain-free

Along the Promenade des Gouverneurs

summer day. The fashion-conscious can check out the Vandoos' (*Vingt-deux*) red tunics and tall beaverskin hats. Before leaving, follow signs to the **Promenade des Gouverneurs**, a panoramic walkway wedged between citadel and cliff, overlooking the St Lawrence.

To move from drum-thumping to breast-thumping, head to **colline Parlementaire**, the hill-top base for provincial legislators. From the fort, follow côte de la Citadelle back to rue St-Louis. Turn left and walk through the gates. Parliament is immediately on your right. Since Confederation in 1867, when Québec City became the provincial capital, legislators have met at **Hôtel du Parlement**, at avenue Dufferin and Grande Allée Est. The **Assemblée Nationale's** chambers are rich with gilded woodwork, coats-of-arms and portraits. Guided tours in English and French begin at Door 3 (June 24 to early September: Monday–Friday 9am–4.30pm, weekends 10am–4.30pm; September to June: Monday–Friday 9am–4pm). Cool off in the fragrant gardens, then eat in the stunning *beaux-arts* dining room at **Le Parlementaire** (weekdays 8am–3pm), if you are here at lunchtime and are not planning to eat later in the Grande Allée.

From here, walk across Grande Allée to the **Parc des Champs de Bataille** (National Battlefields Park). In 1759, after a three-month bombardment, the city's topography proved fatal during an attack by British soldiers. Protected by cannon high on Cap Diamant, residents thought they were safe. The British, however, attacked not by water, but by land – from the Plains of Abraham. (The name is not apocalyptic, though francophones say the battle was. The field was named after a wealthy farmer, Abraham Martin, who died long before the British arrived.) Anticipating attack elsewhere, the French rushed into battle without a Plan B. The city fell in 20 minutes, as did the opposing generals, Wolfe and Montcalm.

Today, the battlefield is a 107-ha (250-acre) park, full of winding paths and sunken gardens, where families picnic and lovers stroll. Look for 22 types of cannons, and a few stray cannon balls. Plaques identify the bloody past, and highlight a few ironies. For example, although many francophones revere this site as the birth-

Relics of the battlefield

place of the *souverainiste* (separatist) movement, it was here that Canada's national anthem, 'O Canada,' was first performed.

Walk south on avenue Georges-VI past the bandshell to the **Musée du Québec** on the battlefield grounds (June 1 to early September: daily 10am–5.45pm, Wednesday 10am–9.45pm; early September to end-May: Tuesday to Sunday 11am–5.45pm, Wednesday until 8.45pm), 1 avenue Wolfe-Montcalm. The province opened this museum in 1933 to highlight *Québécois'* achievements. Its 18,000 works range the world, though many of the artists are local celebrities: Marc-Aurele Fortin, Paul-Emile Borduas, Jean-Paul Riopelle, Alfred Pellan. On the ground floor, don't miss *L'Apothéose de Christophe Colomb,* a splendid mural uniting such unlikely characters as Copernicus and George Washington. On the same floor, head to the **Parc des Champs-de-Bataille Centre d'Interprétation** (May to September, daily 10am–5.30pm; September to May, 11am–5.30pm, closed Monday). Here, in 45 minutes, you can re-enact Québec's crucial conquest, with only video and headset for weapons.

From here, it's a short walk down avenue Wolfe-Montcalm to **Grande Allée**, where you can dine *en plein air* at the converted mansions of timber and railroad tycoons. This is one of Québec's most historic roads – trod by fur trappers and traders, rogues and conquerors, paraders and party-goers. Two blocks of continuous cafés and restaurants, small hotels and big umbrellas, are touted as French Canada's *Champs Elysées.* Here you can eat – small or large, plain or fancy, quick-snack cheap or *haute-cuisine* costly. One kilometer (½ mile) to the north, Grande Allée ends at the familiar Porte St-Louis, with a chance for yet one more photo.

Here you can hail a horse-drawn *calèche,* which is guaranteed to clop through the old city at the perfect leisurely pace on command: 'hue! dia!' Or head to the old port for cruises, lasting between one

and eight hours long, departing from the **Lévis Dock** at the end of rue du Marché Champlain. To cross to the south shore, you can take a 10-minute ferry ride and discover the most wonderful view of the city's skyline. Ferries run every 30 minutes during the day, every hour in the evening (tel: 418 644-3704). You could do a round-trip, but beware of Madame La Corriveau. She was hanged for killing her husband, and although her body disappeared, legend has it that her spirit still hovers hereabouts.

Hail a calèche

3. Ile d'Orléans

If you have a day to spare, take a trip to the lovely Ile d'Or-léans and discover a well-preserved slice of rural Québec only 15 minutes from the city. If you want to have dinner at **Le Moulin de St-Laurent** in St-Laurent, make reservations in advance (tel: **418 829-3888**).

Take Route 440 north along the St Lawrence until it merges with Highway 40. Two kilometers (1½ miles) further on is **Pont de l'Ile**, the bridge that leads to **Ile d'Orléans**, where you will find more *vieux* than in *Vieux-Québec*. Be warned: on warm weekends, you might get slowed by sightseers clogging the only bridge to the island, so make this a week-day trip if possible. Once across, head to **chemin Royal** (Route 368), first laid in 1744, a winding two-lane drive around the island (34km/21 miles long, 8km/5 miles wide). Ile d'Orléans is dotted with old farmhouses with mansard tin roofs, old cottages with wrap-around porches, and old churches – centuries-old stone churches *everywhere* you look – once the center of life, and still the center of town.

Along a perimeter road (67km/41 miles) that you can track in less than an hour, discover the province's pioneer style. Many of the island's 7,000 year-round residents claim as ancestors French colonists who came from Normandy and Brittany in the 1640s. Now, as then, they cluster in six villages, often in the same steep-roofed houses held in the family for generations. Their passion for preservation is clear. To control the invasion of modern houses, the province declared the island an historical district in 1970. Take

Île d'Orléans
5 km / 3 miles

time to savor it. Proceed slowly, stopping to admire the flow of *le fleuve* (the river) and buy juicy berries, maple *sirop*, and grilled cobs of sweet corn at roadside stalls.

If you turn left onto Route 368, otherwise known as chemin Royal, you will first come to **St-Pierre**, a town that – like many others here – claims the oldest church in the province. This one was built in 1717. Among the town's monuments to founding families you will find the grave of Felix Leclerc, the father of Québec folk songs. Algonquin Amerindians called the Ile d'Orléans *Minigo*, an enchanted place. Midnight revels give it a rather sinister label: the Ile aux Sorciers. Yet perhaps Leclerc's poem says it best: 'Forty-two miles of tranquility.'

From here on, towns compete church-for-church in beauty and

Stop to buy local fruit

antiquity. **Ste-Famille**, the island's oldest parish, founded in 1661, claims a significant 17th-century sculpted vault with a night sky.

Continue on Route 368 to St-François, where you can climb an observation tower for stunning views of the banks of land on either side. From here, the next village of note is **St-Jean**, once the island capital. Look out on your right for the Manoir Mauvide-Genest (open from late May to mid-October, tel: 418 829-2630; call for opening hours), 1451 chemin Royal, tel: 418 829-2630. Touch the scars on the outer walls of this 1734 mansion, mementoes of British cannon shells that couldn't penetrate the 1-m (3-ft) thick walls. Now a restaurant with a museum upstairs and shop down, it's stuffed with antique Québecois furniture and English porcelain. More modest houses nearby feature attractive wrought-iron sea signs lovingly crafted by land-bound sailors.

To leave the villages that hug the shore, take the route du Mitan across the island, following a path once cut by sleighs and skis, horses and buggies, 8km (5 miles) back to the bridge. Nearby fields earn the area the nickname 'potato kingdom.' For the full circle stick to Route 368 through to **St-Laurent**, where you will cross one of the island's few junctions, at chemin Royal and route des Prêtres, the priests' road. Priests and parishioners of two villages once convened here to settle a dispute over holy relics. Even now, eight churches, more than a dozen processional chapels, and 20 wayside crosses stand as witnesses to the island's history. St-Laurent was formerly the home of sailors and

Ile d'Orleans cemetery

Montmorency Falls

shipbuilders, and you can still see flat-bottomed *chaloups* dry-docked in Parc maritime de St-Laurent (mid-June to early September: 10am–5pm), 120 chemin de la Chalouperie.

In St-Laurent, French and regional cuisine are served at **Le Moulin de St-Laurent** (754 chemin Royal, tel: 418 829-3888). Open from May to October, this converted flourmill that was built in 1725 offers delightful views from its patio over the waterfall, and live music on weekends.

Continue on to Ste-Pétronille, with its church that was built by Huron converts to Christianity as a sanctuary from the Iroquois. In the 1800s, wealthy Canadian and American visitors favored this town with showy Regency-style summer homes. Here steamships dropped summer visitors before a bridge finally linked boat-weary islanders to Québec City in 1935.

As you backtrack over the bridge, heading back towards the city, look out for **Montmorency Falls**, tumbling 84m (274ft) – as guides will tell you, this waterfall is 30m (100ft) higher than Niagara. What you won't hear from them is this: the falls are *much* narrower, and provincial party-poopers have introduced admission charges and parking fees at this perennially popular picnic spot, officially called **Parc de la Chute-Montmorency** (open all year round, day and night). It is probably worth the fee if you are going to participate: take time to get sprayed by the gushing water – protective rainwear is available – ride the cable car (for a further small charge), cross the 19-m (60-ft) suspension bridge, and explore the historic British encampments.

If you are visiting the falls in the winter, you may see climbers hacking their way down the ice-covered cliff. When the river freezes at the foot of the falls, ice piles into a 'sugarloaf.' Here, in 1820, *Québécois* carvers created a meeting room inside the ice cone, which should have cooled even the most heated arguments.

Just as Québec is distinct in Canada, so Montréal is distinct in Québec. Forget that the city isn't even the capital of its own province, it acts as if it heads a nation. Indeed, as any of its million citizens will boast, Montreal really is *le monde*.

The two tours of Montréal that follow aim to guide you quickly and efficiently to the main sights. The first itinerary is a walk around the old city; the second is a Metro-hopping tour of the city's other points of interest, including the Parc du Mont-Royal, the Olympic Stadium and the Musée des beaux arts.

To get around the city, rely on its excellent Metro and your feet. Go slowly, and indulge your curiosity. Don't hesitate

Saying 'Bonjour'

to turn a two-hour jaunt into a four-hour stroll, with plenty of stops for refreshment. In Montréal, you'll find something for every taste.

4. Le Vieux-Montréal

Discover Montréal by entering its heart. Start by visiting the Musée d'archéologie et d'histoire de Montréal and the old port in Le Vieux-Montréal, then have a look at some of the city's most interesting old buildings. Explore the ethnic districts around boulevard St-Laurent, then take in some contemporary art or an avant garde film. A full-day tour. See map on page 32.

Your starting point is Place d'Youville. From Square Victoria Metro, walk downhill on rue McGill and turn left onto the plaza. Head four blocks to **Pointe-à-Callière**, **Musée d'archéologie et d'histoire de Montréal** (Tuesday to Friday 10am–5pm; weekends 11am–5pm; July and August 10am–6pm), 350 Place Royale. An underground-and-above network of informative fun, the museum combines new exhibition hall, old plaza, and middle-aged customs house.

Exhibits at Pointe-à-Callière

Start with 16-multi-media-filled minutes learning about Montréal's birth and adolescence. Next head downstairs to the 'crypt,' named for its depth, low ceilings, and graves unearthed during excavation. As you meander from one uncovered foundation to the next,

one century to another, virtual figures talk about their lives. Follow the path to the stairs to the 1838 customs building, now a bookstore and gift shop. Once outside, check how you passed under **Place Royale**, former market-place and the city's founding site in 1642.

During the 17th and 18th century, Montréal, like Québec City, was fortified, initially with wood, then with thick stone walls. Nestled in narrow walkways, houses date back more than 300 years, among the oldest in North America. The lives of their early occupants were regulated by religious, administrative, and economic institutions whose edifices still stand.

Follow rue de la Commune northeast along **promenade du Vieux-Port**. Trappers, Indians and merchants once haggled over furs in these stone warehouses. Stretching 2.5km (1½miles) along the St Lawrence river, the docks still bustle with boats.

Protector of sailors

Water taxis have replaced schooners stuffed with New World furs and fish, but the streets are as crowded as they were 200 years ago. It's now a waterfront park with entertainment and exhibits, bicycle paths and picnic spots – spiffed up since the city's 350th anniver-

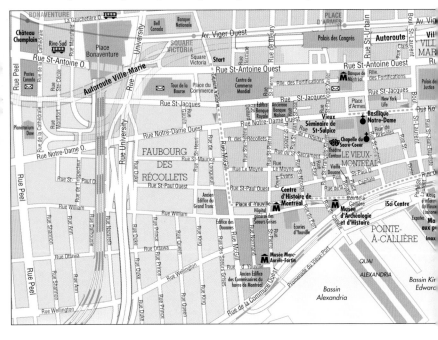

Mime artist in action

sary in 1992. In summer, the promenade is awash with water-mad Montréalers who come to stroll or cycle, lounge or table-hop.

Almost everything floats here: flat-bottomed boats, a New Orleans paddlewheeler, water scooters headed to the Lachine Rapids, shuttles enroute to Parc des Iles, romantic cruises for an hour or a day. On King Edward Pier the new Montréal Interactive Science Centre is commonly referred to as the **iSci Centre**. This vast science and entertainment complex, including an IMAX theater, makes all the science, technology and innovations that affect our lives more understandable, as well as fun, through interactive exhibits and an interactive cinema where you get to play director (daily, 10am–10pm; mid-June to early September, 10am–midnight). For another perspective on the crowds (and calm), walk northeast to the **Tour de l'horloge**, a 45-m (147-ft) clocktower that offers views wide and romantic. Climb and pay homage to today's port to the northeast, where container ships keep the city's maritime heritage alive. Now follow in the footsteps of thousands of sailors. Walk up rue Bonsecours to **Chapelle de Notre-Dame-de-Bon-Secours** (May to October: Tuesday to Sunday 10am–5pm; November to April: Tuesday to Sunday 11am–3.30pm), 400 rue St Paul est. One of the oldest churches in the city, this octagonal building, built in 1771 upon the foundations of the city's first stone church (built in 1675) is strewn with model ships left by sailors grateful to be on land.

Continue southwest on winding **rue St-Paul**, designed in 1672 as Montréal's Main Street. Still active, the street offers eateries, gift shops and boutiques. At **Place Jacques Cartier**, street artists paint near

Old Montréal
200 m / 220 yds

rue St-Amable and perform near the 18th-century buildings that border the sloping walkway.

Anchoring the south plaza, a controversial pink granite monument honors the city's 350th anniversary.

As you climb uphill, look up at Admiral Horatio Nelson, a towering oddity that is Montréal's oldest monument. Walk up to the high side of the plaza for a view of the **Hôtel de Ville**, the Second Empire city hall at 275 rue Notre Dame est. In 1967, French president Charles de Gaulle fueled *souverainiste* aspirations when he shouted '*Vive le Québec libre*' ('Long live free Québec') from the central balcony. The balcony has been closed ever since.

Walk two blocks east along rue Notre Dame est to the **Maison du Sir George-Étienne Cartier**, the double-duty house of a Québec statesman and nation-builder (April 7 to June 22 and September 1 to December 19: Wednesday to Sunday 10am–noon, 1pm–5pm; June 24 to August 29: daily 10am–6pm; closed: January–March), 458 Notre Dame est, tel: 283-2282. Be an intruder, eavesdropping as butlers and maids gossip about the family.

Backtrack along Notre Dame to **Place d'Armes**, a serene square with a turbulent past. Here Iroquois battled settlers, Americans battled British, *patriotes* battled Tories. The monument in the square's center recalls much of this, plus Paul de Chomedey, Sieur de Maisonneuve, the city founder who arrived with colonists and the cross. Surrounded by some of Montréal's most impressive architecture, the square is quiet today. Check out the head office of the **Banque de Montréal**, Canada's first chartered bank (banking hours only), 119 rue St Jacques ouest. Walk through the mock-Romanesque lobby – restored to its 1905 glamor – to a tiny museum where mechanical banks charm tykes and tycoons alike.

Across the way, you won't miss **Basilique Notre-Dame**, one of Canada's first Gothic Revival churches, (June 24 to Labor Day: daily 8am–8pm; otherwise until 6pm), which dominates the square. Twin towers, Temperance and Perseverance, loom 69m (227ft). Inside, color bursts over the altar like fireworks. With gallery seats, carved wainscoting and lavish gilt, the basilica reminds music lovers of opera house grandeur. The Montréal Symphony sometimes performs here. Check for concerts.

Vieux Séminaire de St Sulpice next door is said to be the city's oldest building. Built between 1684 and 1687, it housed Sulpician priests, once the island's largest landowners. Now hail a *calèche* (horse-drawn carriage). You will find one outside the basilica or in Place Jacques Cartier. Ask for **boulevard St-Laurent** or **rue St-**

Denis. En route, listen for rowdy *chansonnière* singing at *boîtes-a-chanson*, then sit back and hum along as Montréal bumps by.

When you alight from your carriage you will find that, although quite close together, these two popular and populous north-south streets are many ethnic kilometers apart. St-Laurent is a Babel of immigrant voices, *Québécois oui*s, Canadian yahoos. St-Denis is *très français*. One shouts and dances; the other shines and dawdles. You could easily spend the rest of the day here.

It is most important that you arrive here hungry. Few places in the city – *mon dieu*, in the world – offer such opportunity to gorge. Bakery follows bistro follows café (see *Eating Out* for details of a few recommended restaurants).

Known as **The Main**, St-Laurent has always been more work-a-day than holiday. Poor immigrants and their richer offspring give the street its flavor, especially strong north of rue Sherbrooke. Here Portuguese cafés, Jewish delis, and Chinese noodle shops entice with long menus and appetizing aromas. Luckily, eating can be cheap, and inhaling is free. Stores are as varied as the food: some rich, some kitsch. Look for smoked meat, funky clothes, and Leonard Cohen, the cult poet-pop singer who lives off the block.

For a chuckle, drop in at the **Musée International de L'humour**, (845-4000) the Just for Laughs Museum, at 2111 Boulevard St Laurent (Thursday and Friday: 9.30am–3.30pm; Saturday and Sunday: 10am–5pm).

Explore the eight blocks north to rue Duluth, then cut east to francophone St-Denis. St-Denis awakens late. Most stores open at 11am, some at noon. Elegant greystones line the wide boulevard.

St-Laurent bakery

Once homes to artists and intellectuals, they now house boutiques, bistros, high-brow bookstores. Cafés fill early with *les Montréalais* people-watching, their favorite sport after hockey. The first patron to go home loses.

Head south on St-Denis, where you can catch *avant-garde* films at **La Cinémathèque Québécoise** (335 de Maisonneuve Est, tel: 514 842-9763) or Canadiana at the ONF/**National Film Board** (1564 St-Denis, tel: 514 496-6887). For more art and culture, take the metro two stops to Place des Arts. Here, along with Picassos and Warhols, the **Musée d'art contemporain de Montréal** presents works of *Québécois* who may once have lived on St-Denis, Tuesday to Sunday, 11am–6pm; free Wednesday 6pm–9pm), 185 Ste-Catherine ouest.

Gallery-goer

Some of Montréal's high points are physically lofty, others metaphorically so. Most half-day bus tours include these on their itinerary, starting at Infotouriste, rue Ste-Catherine and rue Peel, but this tour assumes you will visit them independently, by hopping on and off the Metro – it's not difficult. If you want to make a long day of it, spend the afternoon on swish Sherbrooke ouest and visit the Museum of Fine Arts.

Take the Metro to côte-des-Neiges and head east on the street of the same name, then south on Chemin Queen Mary. Smack en route is the granite and concrete **Oratoire St-Joseph** – known as St Joe's to locals – with a high dome (263m/865ft) that bows only to St Peter's in Rome (summer tours: 1.30pm daily, near the carillons; Way of the Cross in English: Tuesday and Friday, 3.30pm and 8.30pm; museum: daily 10am–5pm; masses from 7am; donations appreciated). This building is the life's work of Blessed Frère André, a humble monk with a reputation for cures that drew pilgrims at the end of the 19th century. Church leaders – first skeptical, then conciliatory – approved construction of the basilica in 1924

Oratoire St-Joseph

to replace the small chapel, overwhelmed by visitors, which previously stood here.

The faithful still flock here, more than 2 million each year, so come early. Some climb the 283 steps to the church on their knees. Others pray at Frère André's tomb, in a passageway lit by votive lights off the main-floor sanctuary. Follow numbered arrows through the cavernous cathedral, among the five largest Roman Catholic shrines in the world, a homage to Canada's patron saint. Upstairs, don't miss the museum where, following a European tradition, the blessed brother's preserved heart is on display. Stolen from near the main altar in 1973, it is now closely guarded. Don't get too close.

From the terrace, you'll discover how **Parc du Mont-Royal** surrounds you, a natural peak of volcanic rock that complements the cathedral's man-made dome. Though only 223m (765ft), this is *la montagne* to proud Montréalers. If you visit the park, wander along zigzag trails and watch locals unwind and the city unfold. Head to the belvedere lookout and the centre de la Montagne information center for guided tours, theme visits,

Le Tour Olympique

and maps (park: daily 6am–midnight; centre: daily, 10am–6pm).

After your visit to the shrine or the park, return to the Metro and take it to Pie IX station, where another high point awaits. At 169m (554ft), **le Tour Olympique** is cited as the world's highest inclining tower (June 15 to September 2: 10am–9pm; rest of the year: 10am–6pm). Ride the funicular up the backbone of this secular spire – inclined 45 degrees – and look across the city. On a clear day you can see for about 80km (50 miles).

Closer, almost beneath your feet, is a giant cyclist's helmet, formed from concrete poured in huge quantities. Built for competitors in the 1976 Summer Olympics, the former velodrome is now **le Biodôme de Montréal** (daily, 9am–5pm; in summer, 9am–7pm), 4777 Pierre de Coubertin. Waterfalls replace Olympic wheels, bird squawks replace bike spokes. Walk through four re-created ecosystems: rain forest, polar ice caps, St Lawrence shore and Laurentian woods. Scientists control humidity, temperature, and soil density, all the while hoping that 4,000 animals and 5,000 plants will call this home. Some forgive the concrete boulders and cement trees; some don't.

For real flowers and trees, walk or take the shuttle north across rue Sherbrooke to **le Jardin Botanique de Montréal** (daily 9am–5pm; in summer 9am–7pm), 4101 rue Sherbrooke est. Second in size only to Kew Gardens near London, this park offers more than 30,000 species of flowers and shrubs to lure strollers, lovers, and bees. Luckily, many bugs are inside, inanimate, at the **Insectarium** nearby. Celebrate spring in these gardens with sprays of cherry blossom, and summer with magnolias. Even when the temperature dips, the 30 gardens and 10 greenhouses make an attractive retreat.

You may like to have a picnic lunch and spend the rest of the day enjoying the botanical garden, but if you have the energy for

Montréal in the fall

more sightseeing, hop back on the Metro at Pie IX and travel a few stops to McGill station, to explore **rue Sherbrooke Ouest**.

Always a wealthy area, this is where the elite once lived and where they still meet and mingle. If you can't act the part, at least act impressed. Located only five minutes west of the McGill Metro, Sherbrooke is a mixture of new, luxury hotels and old graystone mansions. The heart of the Golden Square Mile – home to late-19th-century Montréalers who controlled more than 70 percent of Canada's wealth – these houses are now pricey boutiques and bistros, artsy *ateliers,* and antique shops. Be sure to admire the towers and turrets, and the windows, both bay and bow.

To pay homage to Montréal's, and Canada's, past, head to **Musée McCord, the Museum of Canadian History** (Tuesday to Friday 10am–6pm; Saturday and Sunday 10am–5pm; in summer Monday 10am–5pm), 690 Sherbrooke ouest. With some of his considerable business profits and a sense of *noblesse oblige,* local tycoon David Ross McCord founded a museum housing eclectic displays from many eras. The exhibits include a bust of George III, Victorian valentines, and contemporary totem poles. Amid all this, look out for selections of some 400,000 photographs shot by William Notman and his staff, chronicling the 19th-century life and landscape of Canada and the province.

One of Notman's photographs

Few museums are so worldly, but many are more international. Head to one of them, the **Musée des beaux-arts** (Tuesday to Sunday, 11am–6pm, half-price admission Wednesday 5.30–9pm), 1379 Sherbrooke ouest. Many of the exhibits are world-class: there are works by Chagall, Dalí, and Da Vinci. Canada is well-represented, too, by Riopelle, Lemieux, and the Group of Seven.

More striking than the dimly-lit 1912 main building – all neoclassical marble – is the bright annexe across the street at 1380 Sherbrooke ouest, where you will be wowed by the five-story lobby alone. Climb the odd-spaced stairs to visit exhibitions and the fourth-floor sculpture garden. If you can peel yourself away from the impressive city vistas, don't forget you came to check out the art, which is equally wonderful.

The Laurentians

Les Laurentides, as the Laurentians are known, are Québec's popular *paradis* of clear lakes and wide ski slopes. On Friday afternoons, Montréalers flee to this playground of summer escapes or winter weekends. Follow them on Autoroute 15's fast track north, or the slower Route 117. The first resorts appear about a half hour north of Montréal; by the time you've traveled for an hour and a half, you will reach splendid Mont-Tremblant. If you are gripped by wanderlust, head on to backroads of bumpy gravel, steep hills, sharp curves. But be warned: not every Laurentian town is picturesque. Condo clusters and strip shopping centers are all part of 'country living.' In two days, you can see it all. From an overnight base in Ste-Agathe des Monts, just 103km (64 miles) outside Montréal, no stopping point is more than 45 minutes away.

The Laurentians stretch from Montréal in a line of villages following Canadian Pacific's old *P'tit train du Nord* that once brought revelers 'up north.' Now, as then, the region's *raison d'être* is clear: outdoor fun. This is North America's largest ski village – 150 centers spread over 19 mountains in a 145-km (90-mile) radius.

Almost 300cm (118in) of snow lets you ski, sled, skate, snowboard, snowmobile, even ski-jor behind a plane. If you're a serious athlete, head north, where mountains are steeper. In the social south, look for lift-line *soirées* and night-ski romance (Laurentian Tourist Association, tel: 450 436-8532 for details).

In summer, when the snow melts, you can sail, swim, fish, windsurf, water-ski, canoe, kayak, paddle boats, raft rivers, cruise lakes. Cross-country ski trails beckon summer hikers and bikers. The largest concentration of golf courses in the province feature scenic tees and low green fees. But beware of mosquitoes in May and June.

St-Sauveur: just one of the region's 150 ski centers

Home in St-Saveur

6. Laurentian Towns

A leisurely day's drive linking a selection of Laurentian towns.

For a glimpse of history, start in **St-Jérôme**, off Autoroute 15 on Route 117, where a statue in the park opposite the cathedral honors 'apostle of colonization' Antoine Labelle. In the 1850s, hoping to stop emigration to the US, this priest opened parishes, wrangled a railroad, and convinced authorities to give would-be farmers *les terres en bois debout* – free land with timber still standing. But the sandy soil sustained few crops, and most francophone settlers remained poor.

Continue on Route 117 to Route 364, then head west a few kilometers to **St-Sauveur-des-Monts**, the Laurentian center of strut. More than 40 bars, bistros, cafés and restaurants beckon from rue Principale and rue de la Gare. Meals range from *soupe au pois* (pea soup) and *creton* (pork) to *escargots* and pheasant. In winter, you can watch skiers, snow-mobilers, even snow-boarders vie for space outdoors and fashion supremacy indoors.

From St-Sauveur, stay on Route 117 through Ste-Adèle to **Ste-Agathe-des-Monts**, the region's oldest resort town, rolling over hills and cuddling **Lac des Sables**.

It was more than its location that established Ste-Agathe-des-Monts as one of Québec's first lakeside resorts. The launch of the popular train service, Le P'tit train du Nord, from Montréal in 1892, helped to cement its success. The train service is long gone, but in 1996 the tracks were converted into a 200-km (124-mile) long bicycle path, from St-Jérôme in the south to Mont-Laurier in the north. It makes for easy biking in summer and exhilarating cross-country skiing in winter. Visitors used to come here only in summer, to loll on the beach, and sail on one of the free lakes still open to the public. Circle the H-shaped lake by car or boat, and admire spacious country homes dating from 1890. Cruises

depart from the Main Street pier (May 15 to June 24: 10.30am–3.30pm; June 24 to Labour Day: 10.30am–7.30pm), Les Bateaux Alouette, tel: 819 326-3656. Look out for festivals: *Le nord en fête* in summer and *L'hiver en nord* in winter.

No town is far away, so enjoy a leisurely pace back along Route 117. In **Val David**, craft shops, workshops, and small exhibit halls hug rue de l'Èglise and nearby hillsides, even if the artists prefer to hibernate. You'll find a different kind of art in **Les Jardins de Rocailles**, a peaceful sanctuary with a sculpture garden, a water garden and over 400 perennials at the foot of Mont-Césaire (June 12 to September 6, concerts on weekends from mid- July onwards; tel: 819 322-6193), 1319 rue Lavoie.

Finding something good to eat is no problem wherever you stop in the Laurentians. You can munch hearty, moderately-priced *habitant* breakfasts all day at Rôtisserie au Petit-Poucet, at 1030 Route 117 near Val David (tel: 819 322-2246), or, at the other end of the gastronomic scale, indulge in fine French cuisine at L'Eau à la Bouche in **Ste-Adèle**, 3003 blvd Ste Adèle, tel: 450 229-2991. Alternatively enjoy Swiss cuisine at Au Mazot Suisse, 5320 blvd Labelle, **Val Morin (**tel: 450 229-5600).

You can also sip wine and tour the *cave à vin* with 32,000 bottles at Le Bistro à Champlain, 75 chemin Masson, **Ste-Marguerite du-Lac-Masson,** tel: 450 228-4988. And when you get to your overnight stop in Ste-Agathe-des-Monts, Chatel Vienna, 6 rue Ste-Lucie, tel: 819 326-1485, awaits you with Austrian specialties.

7. Mont-Tremblant

This tour explores some of the natural attractions of the Laurentians, centered around Mont-Tremblant.

Today, make an early start and head to the old-style Laurentians, where woods, lakes, and turbulent streams engulf the Canadian Shield. Follow Route 117 north 30km (18 miles) to **St-Jovite**, where you can stop for a coffee and a snack at one of the outdoor eateries on rue Ouimet. If you're lucky, musicians will serenade you while you eat.

Ten kilometers (6 miles) further north, confusion! 'Mont Tremblant' – or just 'Tremblant' – identifies a lake, a park, a village, a resort, a mountain range, but no single *mont*. The name comes from the Amerindians who were fearful of Manitou, the lo-

Summer pursuits

Winter wonderland

cal spirit, who grumbled and rumbled, making mountains tremble. (Today, you're more likely to tremble from cold as temperatures here dip lower than at Canadian ski resorts out west. To make sure you're well prepared, consult the Polar Bear Club, 930 Route 117, tel: 450 227-4616).

The village of Mont-Tremblant is home to two venerable resorts. Located on Lac Ouimet, the **Auberge Gray Rocks** revels in history (tel: 800 567-6767 or 819 425-2771). The 90-year-old hotel offered the first ski lesson, packaged the first ski week, and opened the first golf course. Since 1924, the resort has maintained its own airport for hydroplanes and ultra-lights.

Nearby is mammoth **Tremblant**, a resort with 92 trails and a gourmet restaurant, Le Grand Manitou, that draws the Lycra-clad from other provinces and the US (tel: 800 461-8711 or 819 681-2000). Massive renovations have resulted in it becoming acclaimed for much more than downhill skiing. The resort also leases slope-space from **Parc du Mont-Tremblant**, created circa 1900 for year-round recreation (tel: 800 461-8711 or 819 688-2281). From the village, follow Route 327 east, then north, to the entrance. Its 1,248 sq km (482 sq miles) features 405 lakes and seven rivers, plus forests that are home to both mink and moose. In summer, climb the 935-m (3,065-ft) Johansen and explore 400km (248 miles) of trails on foot, horseback, or bike. In winter, join cross-country skiers gliding along 170km (105 miles) of trails, offering bunkhouses for overnight stays. Nearby, but separate, are 75km (47 miles) of snowmobile trails which follow along the Trans-Canada route.

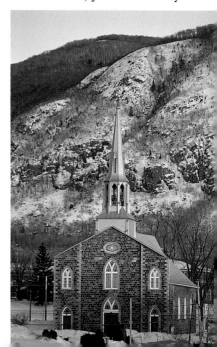

From here, depending on the season and on how much time you have, you can either head south to Montréal, around 90 minutes (140km/87miles) away, or head north to the Hautes Laurentians (higher still) for hunting and fishing, where trips are often guided by local Amerindians who are descendants of the area's first intrepid tourists.

Christmas card scenery

The Eastern Townships

The countryside in Québec's Cantons-de-l'Est (Eastern Townships) can best be described as bucolic. In winter, low mountains catch the hearts of skiers. In summer, browsers follow cart and car tracks in search of clean air, fresh fruit, new crafts, old furniture. To see it all, you'll need a car, unless you're a competent-enough cyclist to pedal on hilly roads. (You can rent bicycles in most towns.) Within just an hour's drive of downtown Montréal, the Townships best distill the province's quirky blend of British and French. Thanks to British Loyalists who fled here after the American Revolution, villages at first seem more American Yankee than Canadian French. White clapboard houses and tidy picket fences shape the towns. Covered bridges and round barns, first built in Massachusetts, dot the valleys. But appearances are deceptive: it was the French who built the railroads and exploited the forests, dominating the region by the late 1800s.

Country living

This section of the guide comprises two full-day tours of the Eastern Townships designed to be followed sequentially but perfectly possible singly. Book accomodation in Lac-Brome/Knowlton for the first night, and in North Hatley for the second, if you plan to make both trips. Motel Cyprès Lac Brome (tel: 450 243-0363) is recommended for the former, and Cedar Gables (tel: 819 842 4120) for the latter.

To reach the region from Montréal, leave the island over the Champlain Bridge and continuing east on Autoroute des Cantons-de-l'Est (Autoroute 10E). The townships lie about 80km (50 miles) east of Montréal, about 100km (62 miles) south of Québec City.

8. Wine Trail

A tour through the Eastern Townships, beginning at Bromont. Opportunities to visit vineyards, ride a horse or llama, visit a monastery and sample regional cooking. Book ahead for lunch in one of the vineyard restaurants (*see below*).

At **Bromont**, you could tackle what townshippers do best: ride horseback on trails that snake 200km (124 miles) throughout the region. For beginners, Centre Equestre Bromont, site of the 1976 Olympic equestrian events, offers lessons (100 rue Laprairie, tel: 450 534-3255, located off chemin Gaspé).

Limit your ride to an hour or two – which will probably be enough, unless you are a very experienced rider – then head deeper

into the townships, driving south on Route 241. This is farm country, so let your pace reflect that. Investigate roadside vegetable stands and at-home art galleries. Fill up on strawberries in June, raspberries in July, and blueberries in August. Return to Route 241 and drive to Route 104. If you're willing to go slightly out of the way, you will discover some treats.

Follow Route 104 west through Cowansville and connect with Route 202. Here, *les vignobles* growers produce whites, reds, and *rosés* from vines near **Dunham** that are hardy enough to withstand six months of winter. Many vineyards organize *dégustations* on weekends in spring and late fall, and daily during summer and the September harvest (usually 10am–5pm; sometimes there is a small charge). A few of them open restaurants in summer and fall, for which reservations are a must.

Sun worshipper

Look for Vignoble Les Blancs Côteaux, 1046 chemin Bruce, Route 202 (tel: 450 295-3503), Vignoble de l'Orpailleur, 1086 Route 202 (tel: 450 295-2763), and Vignoble Domaine Côtes d'Ardoise, 879 Rte 202 (tel: 450 295-2020).

If you prefer fresh fruit to wine, it's only a short drive west from Dunham on the chemin des Vins to find first-rate apples. During the fall, trees near **Stanbridge East** are loaded with delicious fruit in U-Pick fields.

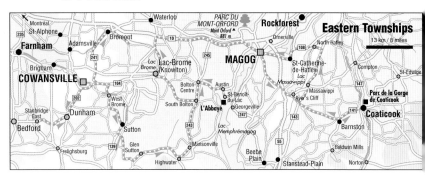

Spring blossom: a special attraction of the Eastern Townships

Back where the 241 and 104 intersect, head east 6km (4 miles) to Route 139. From here, it's about 10 minutes south to **West Brome**, where a general store, Magasin F G Edwards at 12 McCurdy, is authentically rustic, offering milk buckets, horse harnesses, and lumberjack shirts for sale. About 20 minutes further along Route 139 is **Sutton**, a small town rich in history and crafts. First settled in 1795, the village bustles today – in winter, when glade skiers tackle nearby **Mont Sutton**; in summer, when artists and antique dealers beckon; in between, when the spring blossom and fall foliage are enough to attract visitors.

Abandon your car for a while. Rent a llama for a trek at Llamadu, 1333 chemin Jordan, tel: 450 538-5521 (mid-May to late October: daily 10am–5pm). During the Tour des arts each July, as many as 40 art and craft studios in the vicinity are open to visitors following a map *à la* treasure hunts. If you didn't eat at one of the vineyard restaurants, you can nibble *crudités* at La Fontaine, 38 Principale Sud (tel: 450 538-3045) or vegetarian specials at Resto Belvue, 381 Route 139 North (tel: 450 538-2220). But save room for dessert at René Henquin's Centre d'interpretation du Chocolate, 8 Principale sud.

Circular barn

A Belgian chocolate-maker offers four interesting demonstrations daily, June to October (tel: 450 538-0139 for times).

Now be prepared for some of Mont Sutton's heart-stopping views and altitudes. Follow Route 139, turning left onto Rue Brookfall and immediately right onto **chemin Scenic** along Route 105A. This 40-minute drive carries you past mountain panoramas and through peaceful villages, Glen Sutton to Highwater. Here, turn north onto Route 243 to **Mansonville**, where a circular barn is tucked across from the Catholic church. Peek inside. First designed by Shakers, these barns allow no corners for devils to hide. Next, look out for a covered bridge, another local attraction. For an interesting detour, turn right onto rue Vale Perkins and follow the signs to rue Belle-vue. But beware! Dirt roads can turn muddy. Follow signs up to St-Benoît-du-Lac. Otherwise, continue on Route 243 to South Bolton, then pick up Route 245. Look for the local landmark at the intersection: a white-and-blue rocket mounted diagonally, cast off from a defunct restaurant. Stop in at **Bolton Center** for Mediterranean cuisine at L'Iris Bleu, Route 245 (tel: 450 292-3530).

For really heavenly food, follow signs to Austin, then to **L'Abbaye-de-St-Benoît-du- Lac**, perched majestically on land jutting into

Lac Memphremagog – aptly, this is Abenaki for 'very extensive lake.' Original Indian names still abound – Massawippi and Coaticook are situated further along this route, for instance – and no one even attempts French translations.

Founded in 1912, the granite, hilltop monastery on chemin des Pères is tranquil home to 60 Benedictine monks who produce cider, two well-regarded cheeses (L'Ermite and Mont St Benoît), and haunting chants that float over surrounding fields. Recordings are available in the gift shop, alongside apple sauce, caramels, and chocolate spreads (abbey: daily 8am–8pm; gift-shop: November to May, Monday to Friday 9–10.45am and 1.30–4.30pm; Saturday 9–10.45am and 11.45am–4.30pm. June to October, Monday to Saturday 9–10.45am and 11.45am–4.30pm. July and August 11.45am–6pm, closed Sunday; eucharist: daily 11am; vespers: daily 5pm, except Thursday

In memory of a moose

7pm and Tuesday, July to August; tel 819 843-4080).

In July, look for long-distance swimmers plowing through the water from the lake's southern end in Vermont to its northern reach 42km (26 miles) away in Magog. Entertained by parachute jumps during the day and bonfires at night, 20,000 spectators cheer on the contestants in the Lac Memphremagog International Swim Marathon, who often swim more than 18 hours to finish.

Head to **Lac-Brome**, still called **Knowlton** by locals. Because French names are more popular with politicians than township-pers, the region may be Québec's most tolerant and bicultural. Transformed from faded resort to bustling craft center, Lac-Brome now spreads its shops along chemin Lakeside and chemin Knowl-ton: antique to *avant garde*, hokey to chic, dangling flower baskets to customized wood signs. Here, you'll find items once exclusive to urban outlets, plus English woolens and French porcelain.

Lakeside refreshment

Plan to spend the night here (you should have made reservations), but enjoy dinner first. If you can manage it after Swedish meatballs at Nilsson's, 70 chemin Lakeside (tel: 450 243-0621), try Swedish cinnamon cake with fresh whipped cream. For lighter fare, head to the Knowlton Pub at 267 chemin Knowlton (tel: 450 242-6862), famous for tasty French fries and smoked meat sandwiches. Check for English productions next door at Théâtre du Lac-Brome (mid-June to mid-September, Tuesday to Saturday, plus matinées twice weekly; tel: 450 242-2270 and 242-1395).

9. Parks and Lakes

Picking up where yesterday's itinerary left off, today's tour explores more of the Eastern Townships, including the Parc de la Gorge de Coaticook and Lake Massawippi.

–It's advisable to reserve a table if you want to have dinner at Auberge Hatley (tel: 819 842-2451) or Manoir Hovey (tel: 819 842 2421).–

After a good night's sleep – and some lake views if you stayed at Cyprés Lac Brome – set off for **Parc du Mont-Orford** (April to September: open daily 9am–10pm, October to March: daily 9am–5pm). Drive along Route 243 north to Autoroute 10 and east about 15km (9 miles), to the park entrance near exit 115. Year-round, the 881-m (2,860-ft) mountain welcomes hikers and nature-gazers alike. In wintertime, annual snowfalls of 4.82m (190in) usually ensure skiing from late November to early April.

From the park, head southeast on Route 141. Stop for lunch in Ayer's

Coaticook's suspension footbridge

Cliff. For *haute cuisine*, indulge yourself at Auberge Ripplecove, 700 rue Ripplecove (tel: 819 838-4296). Then follow Barnston to Coaticook, home of **Parc de la Gorge de Coaticook** (May to November: daily 10am–5pm; June 25 to Labor Day: 9am–7pm; rest of the year: Monday to Wednesday 9am–4pm; Thursday to Sunday 9am–9pm), 135 rue Michaud, on the outskirts of town along Route 147. The longest suspension footbridge in the world – 169m (555ft)

Rural idyll

– will swoop you over a gorge that drops 50m (164ft) to the river. The faint-hearted might choose to give this a miss and head for the **Musée Beaulne** (mid-May to mid-September: daily 11am–5pm; July 6 to mid-August, 11am–8pm; mid-September to mid-May: Wednesday to Sunday, 1–4pm), 96 rue Union. This Victorian mansion displays costumes, textiles, and photographic treasures from the 1920s.

Now head north on Route 143 to chemin de Hatley for your overnight stop at **North Hatley**. The village was founded early in the 20th century by wealthy Americans eager to escape humid summers in the American South. Bitter about Civil War losses, these aristocrats pulled down shades on railroad cars as they passed through the Yankee north, and headed across the border. Today, their summer homes on the northern end of the **Lac Massawippi** are bed and breakfasts, shops, and restaurants with choice lakeside views.

Walk along the shores, or row a boat on the lake. Notice oddly warm air? This village is in a peculiar climatic pocket that attracts flora and fauna usually found further south. Roam on, to dawdle over craft, gift and antique shops. Climb two flights of stairs to Galerie d'art naif Jeannine Blais, 100 rue Principale (daily 10am–5pm), 819 842-2784, which specializes in local and international primitive art. An international contest in October attracts painters of bucolic frolics. Check out The Piggery, on Route 108, once accommodation for pigs, now home to actors presenting plays in English (from early July to early September; tel: 819 842-2431).

Characteristic clapboard

For dinner (Wednesday to Saturday at 5.30pm) head to Le Café Massawippi on Capleton Road where locals simply say: 'Feed us' (tel: 819 842-4528). If you are after more formal, three-course, *prix-fixe* dinners, and pricey local specialties such as rabbit, pheasant, or Lac Brome duck, you should reserve at either Auberge Hatley on Route 108 (tel: 819 842-2451) or Manoir Hovey at 585 Chemin Hovey (tel: 819 842-2421). To head back to Montréal take Route 108 west to Ste Catherine-de-Hatley. Midway between Lakes Massawippi and Magog, this small village has one of the most spectacular panoramic views in the Eastern Townships, over Mont Orford and its surroundings. Then continue along Route 112 north to Autoroute 10W.

Charlevoix

Charlevoix stretches along the St Lawrence River's north shore east of Québec City to the Saguenay River. With ice-molded hills and granite-sculpted cliffs, this region offers some of the world's oldest terrain. Here you'll find clapboard houses on the edge of maple forests, squat lighthouses on the edge of ragged cliffs – and whale-watchers on the edge of their seats. This section suggests spending two days in the region, staying overnight in Pointe-au-Pic. The Auberge des Falaises (tel: 418 665-3731 or 1-800-386-3731) or the Auberge des Trois Canards (tel: 418 665-3761 or 1-800-461-3761) are recommended, but you will need to make reservations.

To reach the region of Charlevoix from Québec City leave the city on Route 132 Est.

10. Charlevoix Arts and Crafts

The first day includes a visit to the Basilique Ste-Anne-de-Beaupré before going on to the 300-year-old village of Baie-St-Paul, and the Ile-aux-Coudres, ending the day at La Malbai-Pointe-au-Pic. See map on page 50.

Your first stop is a pilgrimage that some 1.5 million visitors take annually to the **Basilique Ste-Anne-de-Beaupré** (early May to mid-September, daily 8.30am–5pm; September to May, daily but at varying times), 10018 avenue Royale (tel: 418 829-3781). For many centuries, those in search of cures flocked here to honor St Anne, patroness of sailors, as well as of the province. Those who irreverently dub this 'the miracle mart' might hesitate to go further: to the **wax museum** at the basilica's parking lot, to the world's largest religious panorama, dating from 1895, at **Cyclorama de Jérusalem,** 8 rue Regina, or to see the 50 crafted silver panels at **Christorama** (look for the sign 'Copper Studio' or 'Cuivre Albert Gilles'), 7450 Ste-Anne, Château-Richer (tel: 824-4224).

Charlevoix officially starts just past Ste-Anne. Named for New France's first historian, a Jesuit priest, the region was poor in land to farm, but rich in trees to chop and boats

Steeples of Ste-Anne-de-Beaupré

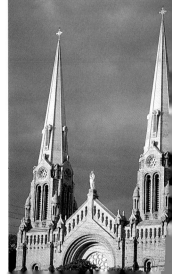

to pilot. Lumberjacks – *gens de hache* – sawed so deep into the region's wild interior that they outpaced progress. Roads didn't reach some spots here until the 1950s. Though you can hug the coast, as settlers did in the 17th century, you do now have roads. If you are traveling this way in May or October, 100,000 snow geese will fly in V-formations for you on their annual migrations at **Cap-Tourmente**.

Charlevoix
16 km / 10 miles

From here, the road winds into villages of white-frame houses and tin-roof churches, past roadside crosses that mark religious roots and routes. Head 50km (31 miles) to **Baie St Paul**, a 300-year-old village nestled in the valley where the Gouffre and St Lawrence rivers meet. Dramatic landscape shaped by meteorites and earthquakes frames extraordinary light that has inspired poets and painters for more than a century. Many of Canada's famous Group of Seven artists regularly stopped at the 1852 farmhouse of painter René Richard. Now the **Maison de René Richard,** it's filled with his bold strokes and dots (daily 10am– 6pm), 58 rue St-Jean-Baptiste.

Do you smell paint and linseed oil? It emanates from the activities of the artists who still live nearby. Oils, acrylics, and watercolors are on view or sale everywhere. Galleries line rue Ambroise Fafard and St Jean Baptiste, alongside some good places to have lunch. Reconnoiter **Centre d'art de Baie-St-Paul** (late June to early September: 9am–7pm; otherwise 9am–5pm), 4 rue Ambroise-Fafard, and **Le Centre d'Exposition** (daily September to June 24, 9am–5pm; daily June 24 to early September, 9am–7pm), 23 rue Ambroise-Fafard.

From early August to early September, **Le Symposium de la Nouvelle Peinture au Canada** puts 15 young artists from Canada and abroad on the public spot, painting at the Centre d'art, in grand style and grand size – 4.6sq m (50sq ft).

But now it is probably time to practice the art of eating. A two-minute

A dab hand at work

walk from Ambroise Fa-fard's intersection with Jean Baptiste brings you to Restaurant Le Mouton Noir, 43 rue Ste-Anne (tel: 418 240-3030), which offers French cuisine in a cozy dining room.

As you leave Baie St-Paul, consider heading north on Route 381 into an interior so magnificent that UNESCO has designated 6,000sq km (3,750sq miles) of it a world biosphere reserve. By car, canoe, or mountain bike, you can tackle the taiga's evergreen swamps or the tundra's treeless plains. If you want to spend some time here and explore the area at length, you can pitch your tent, rent a chalet or stay in a shelter in the **Parc des Grands-Jardins** (in season, tel: 418 846-2057; off season, tel: 418 435-3101).

However, if you are following this itinerary and moving on, follow the scenic coastal Route 362 that winds up a mountain, then plummets to **St-Joseph-de-la-Rive**. Here, boatwrights built more than 300 *goélettes* to haul cargo – from lobsters to lumber – along the coast. At the water's edge, look out for a towering mast stuck in the ground near a white frame office shaped like a tugboat. **Exposition Maritime** (late June to early September: daily 9am–5pm; limited hours the rest of the year), 305 Place de l'Eglise, offers a selection of navigational aids as well as three dry-docked boats to examine. Across the street in a refurbished schoolhouse is **Papeterie St-**

Gilles (open all year round; summer hours, May to November, 8–5pm daily), 304 rue Félix-Antoine-Savard. Watch craftsman using 17th-century techniques to transform cotton pulp into stunning paper. Artists snap up sheets for watercolors, silkscreens, and lithographs, many of which are on sale here. For yourself, or as presents to take home, consider stationery embedded with wild-

Another local craft

flowers that schoolchildren gather in nearby fields.

Head to the harbor along rue du Quai for a free 20-minute ferry ride to **Ile-aux-Coudres**. Named after the hazelnut trees that explorer Jacques Cartier found here, the island served for two centuries as a center of whaling and boat-building. Even now, former sea captains run small inns where you're likely to find such treats as fried smelt, meat pie tourtière, or sugar pies. You face two choices when you land in St Bernard-sur-Mer: left or right. The route (25km/ 16 miles) is circular, so go ahead and enjoy it – hike, bike, or

drive, stopping to ooh at ancient wind-mills, and aah at beached schooners. **Les Moulins de l'Ile-aux-Coudres**, 247 chemin du Moulin, still grind wheat (open late May to mid-October only: June 19 to August 22: 9am–6.30pm; rest of the time 10am–5pm).

Take the ferry back to St-Joseph and continue north on Route 362 through the valley villages of Les Eboulements and St Irénée. If these look picture per-fect, that's because they are. Museums now dicker over Charlevoix landscapes painted here by such prominent Cana-dians as A Y Jackson and Jean-Paul Lemieux. At **Pointe-au-Pic**, Canada's first resort town, tycoons disembarked from yachts and steamships for *plein air* vacations. Visitors as eminent as US Presi-dent William Howard Taft came each summer to stay in manors clustered around the bay. Those homes now serve handsomely as *auberges* and hotels, offering old-fashioned coddling with famous chefs and such modern amenities as whirlpool baths. **Manoir Richelieu** (tel: 800 441-1414), a rambling 405-room stone castle amid man-icured green at 181 Richelieu, is the area's last grand resort hotel. Once *the* haven for the well-to-do, it has been massively renovated and expanded to house a casino run by Loto-Québec. Don't miss twi-light views from the grand swimming pool or the chance to tee off on North America's oldest golf course.

Once known as Murray Bay, nearby **La Malbaie** (which was re-cently amalgamated with Pointe-au-Pic) now sports the 17th-century misnomer attributed to it by explorer Samuel de Champlain when his ship ran aground at this 'bad bay.' The **Musée de Charlevoix** dis-plays folk treasures plus exotic imports brought by navigators (June 24 to September 2: daily 10am–6pm; September 2 to June 24: Tuesday to Friday 10am–5pm, weekends 1–5pm), 1 chemin du

Museum statue Havre. Even the permanent art is legendary. Adam and Eve greet you at the door. The naked statues so alarmed res-idents that each received 'coats' of paint – Amerindian chic, of course. Look for the 25 whimsical saints in-side. St Breast is eighth on the right.

For dinner, the best advice, and food, may be at your doorstep. Inns compete to hire famous chefs to entice residents and non-residents alike. For fabulous French food try either of the places recommended for accommodation: the Auberge des Falaises (18 chemin des Falaises, tel: 418 665-3731) or the Auberge des Trois Canards (49 côte Bellevue, tel: 418 665-3761). For less ex-pensive Italian food, try Restaurant Allegro in La Malbaie (53 rue John Nairn, tel: 418 665-2595).

11. Whale-watching

Today's trip takes you to Tadoussac on a whale-watching expedition, then gives you the choice of returning to your (pre-booked) hotel in Pointe-au-Pic, driving to Québec City (about 216km/134 miles), or carrying on to the Gaspé Peninsula (see itineraries 12 and 13). Come well prepared for your trip to the island: bring a sunhat, a windbreaker, binoculars, and a picnic.

Start very early, and remember to pack your *pique-nique* if you plan to spend the day afloat. More views and villages will greet you as you drive along Route 138 northeast 71km (44 miles) to **Baie-Ste-Catherine**, which stands sentinel on the Saguenay fjord. Carved deep and narrow by glaciers, the fjord's granite walls rise sharply 300m (984ft). Keep alert! Your first whale sightings may come aboard the 10-minute ferry crossing to **Tadoussac** (daytime departures (8am–9pm) approximately every 20 minutes; after 9pm, every 40 minutes, tel: 418 235-4395). Here, where the St Lawrence meets the Saguenay, fresh water mingles with salt, warm with cold, and two tidal streams collide in shoals – a prime environment for the plankton and krill that whales crave. Indeed, more than 10 species of whales roam here, ranging from the migrating 25-m(90-ft) blue to the resident 5-m(17-ft) white beluga.

Head to the harbor if you want to sail for a few hours, or a few weeks (see *Practical Information* section, *pages 87*). You must reserve in advance during high season. Off season, boats will head out on demand, with prices negotiable. Half-day tours seek out whales. Day-long jaunts also sail up the Saguenay. The fjord, more subtle than stunning, is worth seeing, but the whales mustn't be missed. You will appreciate your trip more if you first learn about these behemoths with interactive video and high-tech fun at the **Centre d'interprétation des mammifères marins** (May 15 to June 23 and October: noon–5pm; June 24 to September 30: 9am–8pm), Route du Quai. Examine a skeleton, a preserved fetus, even a model of a 45-ton finback named Grand Galop. For hands-on adventure, touch whale skin and teeth. You won't get this close on the water.

A whale surfaces off Tadoussac

Tadoussac Hotel

Now it's time to cruise. The spectator sport is as mammoth as its targets, with more than 200,000 visitors in summer. From late-May through to mid-October, cruise boats, mock *goélettes*, even water scooters leave from Baie-Ste-Catherine and Tadoussac. In summer, Zodiac rafts fill up as early as 5am, taking up to 15 people each. Other cruises start at 9.45am, and there are frequent departures throughout the day. Look for certified boaters, pledged to observe environmental guidelines. Consider mass transit – boats carrying 400 passengers to avoid sea jams, which are as dangerous to whales as whalers once were.

You almost always spot something. Prime months are July to September, but there's no best time or place. Watch for wet wheezes as whales spout mist. Look for finbacks feeding in pods, minkes moving in tandem. Choppy water may do nothing to improve your skills as a photographer. To prevent getting seasick, it's wise to eat before you sail, but reduce fluids. If you suffer badly from seasickness, it's best to stick to the shore. Head to two observation points in the **Parc marin du Saguenay.** To do this, backtrack to Pointe-Noire at the mouth of the Saguenay in Baie-Ste-Catherine, or head east on Route 138 about 20km (12 miles) to Cap de Bon-Désir in **Grandes-Bergeronnes** marine sanctuary, 498A rue de la Mer. From a vantage point on rocks, from mid-June to mid-October, you can spot seals, whales, and dolphins.

On land, why not abandon your car in Tadoussac and stretch your legs with a walk. Amerindians named this area 'breasts,' and even a cursory look at the landscape will explain why. Follow a footpath up *colline de l'anse a l'eau* (Parc du Saguenay) or check out one of Canada's oldest wooden chapels (1747) on rue du Bord de l'eau. Nearby, in 1941, construction workers dug up Canada's first fur trading post (1599) as they built the white-bright Tadoussac Hotel that now dominates the bay. You can watch, or join in, hang-gliding on the beach or wind-surfing at high tide.

Natural drinking fountain

From here, the choice is yours: you can go back to Pointe-au-Pic (80km/50 miles), or to Québec City (216km/134 miles) or on to the Gaspé Peninsula (see *Itinerary 12, pages 56*) on the St Lawrence's south shore. To cross the river, backtrack west on Route 138 to **St-Siméon** for a ferry to **Rivière-du-Loup** (tel: 418 638-2856). The crossing takes between 65 and 90 minutes, and boats run on a first-come, first-served basis, so you should be at the departure point at least an hour in advance.

Gaspé Peninsula

If you fancy hiking or biking, fossils or fish, or a jaunt along some of North America's most spectacular coastline, the **Gaspé Peninsula** is the place for you. It makes a wonderful great escape. Three times a week, VIA Rail's Le Chaleur leaves Montréal Central Station (tel: 1-800-361-5390) for the town of Gaspé. On the 16-hour ride (starting in the early evening) you cross the peninsula's spine by night and skirt the craggy Atlantic coast by day. Reserve well in advance especially during the summer. Extra passengers may find they land in the glass-domed observation car. Not bad! At dawn, they'll see the most spectacular scenery on offer east of the Rockies.

Alternatively, you can do the journey by bus (up to 14 hours), or drive 700km (435 miles) or 930km (578 miles) from Québec City or Montréal, respectively. Once on the peninsula, a car is indispensable (try Tilden, tel: 418 775-3502, at the Mont-Joli airport). The route set out here describes a circle beginning and ending in Gaspé town. The complete circuit takes between four and five days and has thus been divided into four consecutive tours that can each be managed in a day (they recommend places to stay overnight). The first tour (No. 12) is based in and around the town of Gaspé.

The Gaspé coast at Percé

Forillon Park

12. Gaspé town and Environs

A journey into the wild, beginning in the town of Gaspé. The day will be spent exploring a national park and/or fishing for salmon, so dress appropriately.

The Micmac Indians considered La Gaspésie peninsula *Gaspeg* – the 'end of the world.' For French explorer Jacques Cartier, it was the beginning. In 1534, on his first journey to North America, Cartier planted a wooden cross for France on a promontory where six cast-iron stelae now commemorate his arrival. So start where he did – at the entrance to the town of Gaspé, for centuries a whaling-and-fishing port, now the region's adminis-trative hub. Book overnight accomodation at one of the hotels listed in the *Accommodation* section of *Practical Information* (*page 85*). The Gîte 'La Normande' (tel: 418 368-5468) is a good and inexpensive choice if you want a pool.

To appreciate local lore, head first to **Musée de la Gaspésie** (late June to Labor Day: daily 8.30am–8.30pm; Labor Day to late June: Tuesday to Friday 9am–5pm, Saturday to Sunday 1–5pm), 80 boulevard Gaspé. Photos and artifacts show just how Gaspésians are '*Un peuple de la mer*,' spiritual descendants of hardy Viking and Basque fishermen who first tackled this harsh land.

Much of the land is still untamed, untouched. Mixed forests cover hilly hinterland such as that in **Parc National de Forillon**, about 20km (12 miles) northeast across Gaspé Bay (mid-June to end Au-

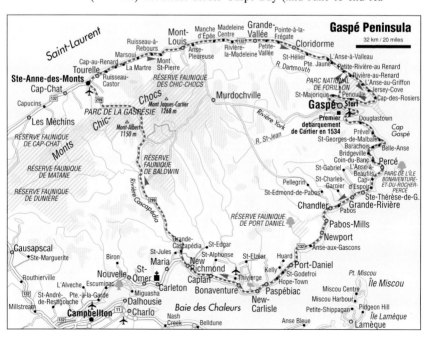

Canada's tallest lighthouse at Cap-des-Rosiers

gust, 9am–6pm; early June and September to mid-October, 10am–5pm), tel: 418 368-5505. Here, you'll find 240sq km (93 sq miles) of limestone cliffs, prairies and dunes, deep-cut coves. You could easily spend a whole day here: hiking, cycling, diving, bird-watching, horseback riding, deep-sea fishing, or tagging along with naturalists. But if time is limited, the least you must do is walk along the cliffs high above Cap Gaspé, where whales frolic.

From Gaspé town, take Route 132 west around the bay to Route 197, a short-cut over the peninsula to the park's northern coast. Once there, head east on Route 132 around the tip of the peninsula, past Canada's tallest lighthouse (37m/136ft) at **Cap-des-Rosiers**. Follow signs to the information center, where detailed explanations of land- and seascapes abound. (Scientists say geology. Amerindians call it The Great Hare.) A few kilometers further on, you can explore stores and homesteads at the late-19th-century Grand-Grave.

If you're back in town at lunchtime, try **Le Bistro Brise-Bise** at 135 rue de la Reine, before you embark on an afternoon's salmon fishing. This, too, could easily be a whole day activity, as there are three rivers brimming with salmon, all within just 16km (10miles)

Try your hand at angling

of Gaspé: York, St-Jean and Dartmouth. Although fishing permits are highly prized, with a little luck you can hook an angling spot (June 1 to September 15; Société de gestion des rivíeres du grand Gaspé, tel: 418 368-2324). Once private playgrounds of the wealthy, in 1978 the Gaspé's rivers were 'de-clubbed' – opened to the public. Now government *zones d'exploitation controllée* (ZECs) control each river's public pools, which are often crowded before daybreak. With dry-fly angling, you may average one salmon every two or three days. Guides or hotels will help you clean and freeze your catch.

All this outdoor activity should have given you a healthy appetite and a good place to satisfy it is **Café des Artistes**, 249 boulevard Gaspé (tel: 418 368-2255) before retiring to your chosen hotel where you have already made reservations.

57

La Rocher Percé

13. Beaches and Birds

Today's tour focuses on the area around Percé, and includes visits to La Rocher Percé and the bird sanctuary on the Ile Bonaventure. Take a windbreaker, sturdy shoes, and binoculars. Book accommodation in Percé before you start. You could try B&B at the Gîte du Capitaine (tel: 418 782-5559), or elegance and *haute cuisine* at the Hôtel La Normandie (tel: 418 782-2112).

If you haven't had breakfast at your hotel, join locals at the Motel Adams, a friendly place at 2 rue Adams, Gaspé (tel: 418 368-2244), then set off for **Percé**, a lively town that fills up fast in summer, especially early July to mid-August, when parking, and even walking, can be a chore. So savor the pastoral peace as you head southeast on Route 132 to Douglastown, past several farms practicing organic agriculture. At **La Ferme Chimo** (mid-June to end August, 9am–4pm; tel: 418 368-4102), located on the highway in Douglastown, you can buy goat's cheese and yogurt from guides who will explain how to manage a goat herd (in case you ever need to know).

Just round a bend aptly named La Côte Surprise, you'll catch your first glimpse of **Rocher Percé,** a limestone colossus, 475m (1,558ft) long, 88m (288ft) high, and more wave-worn than pierced. At 5,000,000 tonnes, this looks like a *very* great ship, mast lost, run aground. After 375 million years, it's down from three arches to one. Get here fast: geologists predict this last one may erode within a few hundred years. As you head into the town, the rock will follow you, visible everywhere, mesmerizing you with colors that change by mood and moment. Much of one day should be spent sidling up to or circling it. First, check tide times posted by merchants or the tourist office, then plan accordingly.

At low tide, you can walk from wood steps at the headland, Mont-Joli. You're on ankle-sprain terrain here, which is why you need sturdy shoes. Tiptoe across a pebbly sandbar, one eye out for crabs, seaworms, and other creepy crawlies. Stick close enough to the rock to avoid falling chips. And, please, don't get stranded by quick-rising water. If you have to wait for low tide, head one mile west of downtown to **Centre d'interprétation du parc de l'Ile**

Bonaventure-et-du-Rocher-Percé for exhibits and slide shows about local flora and fauna (early June to mid-October: daily 9am–5pm), rang de l'Irlande. Or you could have a leisurely lunch at one of the small eateries clustered on promenade du Bord de Mer.

Plan to cast off. Your target is **Ile Bonaventure**, 3km (2 miles) long, a one-time pirate hideaway, now a treasure trove of birds. Choose your boat from the fleet at the downtown dock. If the water is choppy, you might not see anything exceptional from a glass-bottomed catamaran – except the diver sent below to wave. In peak season, boats complete 50 trips, and carry 2,600 visitors. You can buy full-price tickets on the spot or discounted ones at hotels. If you plan to spend the afternoon afloat, and didn't pack a picnic, buy a boxed lunch at La Bôite a Lunch Les Été, 155 Place du Quai, in the gray clapboard mini-mall. If you have time, dash up the gangplank to **Musée Le Chafaud**, modeled on property of the long-time cod-fishing bosses of the Charles Robin Company (early June to late September: daily 10am–10pm), 145 rue Principale.

Now climb aboard. You'll circle Percé rock and discover **Parc de l'Ile Bonaventure**, North America's largest bird sanctuary. More than 250,000 birds engulf the clifftop – puffins, cormorants, kittiwakes, common murres, and the world's largest gathering of gannets. Many arrive in April or May; some stay until October, with rituals of courtship and breeding to entertain you. From the boat, you can watch them dive for fish, squid, and seaweed, hurtling 122m (400ft). When the boat lands, naturalists lead hikes lasting about 60 to 90 minutes each. Along the way, plants vary from arctic to tropical in an environment so fragile that no one is allowed to stay overnight. Thick moss muffles all sound until the last stretch. Then squawks assail you, as do acrid smells (*guano*, otherwise known as bird droppings, in very large quantities).

Back in Percé, the tourist office claims: 'We have something for everybody.' And they do, offering every imaginable way to explore the area, from two-legged to four-wheel. If you want a break from the sea, follow the Mont-Ste-Anne path to a nearby cave (45 minutes) or rue des Failles to earthquake crevasses (60 minutes).

Along the town's *rue principale*, merchants may divert your attention. To take advantage of a short season, boutiques often stay open until 10pm. Recover from your excursions with afternoon tea from 4–5pm at Hôtel la Normandie, 221 Route 132. From the terrace, you can watch wheeling birds, the ancient rock, and the sunset. Check out the dinner menu at the same time, or head uphill to Restaurant Le Gargantua, 222 rue des Failles (tel: 418 782-2852), where all meals come with periwinkle, tasty mini-molusc.

Parc de l'Ile Bonaventure

The third leg of the tour takes in attractive fishing ports, the town of Bonaventure and the Parc de la Gaspésie. Book accomodation in a cabin at the Gîte du Mont-Albert, inside the park (tel: 418 763-2288/888-270-4483).

Set out from Percé on Route 132. South at **L'Anse-à-Beaufils**, the first of many small fishing ports that will seduce you, scour the beach for agates and jaspers. To really get a feel for this peninsula, dawdle on the docks, chat with locals, slow to the rhythm of village life. As early as the 1760s, more than 800 *gaspésiennes* cruised for cod here. But a ban on cod fishing is now forcing unemployed fishermen to re-define themselves. No longer *mangeurs de morue,* a barb recollecting those centuries of fishing, many Gaspésians hope to save their culture by sharing it with tourists. Pride is evident in town after town. Homes are well-

Fisherwoman

tended, mint green shutters tidy against white shingles. Lobster traps are neatly stacked along the quays.

Follow Route 132 to the 'Canadian Riviera' on the **baie des Chaleurs**, where sandy spits and warm water drew both shipwrecked immigrants and wealthy yachtsmen. Scan the horizon for the square-rigged pirate ship once chased from Percé. Legend says it still sails, despite the shells of a French warship. Acadian history and culture pervade **Bonaventure**. Expelled from Acadia (Nova Scotia) by the British in the mid-1700s, francophones fled throughout the territory, and this was one of the places where they ended up.

Explore archival photos and artifacts at the **Musée acadien du Québec** (late June to early Sepember: daily 9am–8pm; early Septem-

Gaspésians pride themselves on their neat homes and towns

ber to mid-October: 9am–5pm; the rest of the year: Monday to Friday 9am–noon, 1–5pm; Saturday to Sunday 1–5pm), avenue 95 Port-Royal. 'First-person' accounts tell a familiar story of the harsh lives of people who survived as fisher-farmers in summer, and hunter-trapper-loggers in winter.

Loyalists fleeing the American Revolution in the 1780s claimed unsettled and unregulated land here, naming Oak Bay, Hope Town, Carleton. But cultural twists are tricky. Intermarriage has turned the surname McInnis respectably francophone. But New Carlisle, home of late *Québécois* firebrand premier René Lévesque, occasionally flies the Union Jack. At **New Richmond**, the **Centre de l'héritage britannique de la Gaspésie** (mid-June to early September: daily 9am–6pm) preserves anglophone traditions and geneaology (351 Perron Ouest). Set on a former air strip of 32ha (80 acres), the village explores how the first English Protestant immigrants thrived beside French Catholic Acadians. Among 20 buildings, ranging from the 17th to 20th century, is the Willett house, where attendants in authentic period costume offer typical British fare: beef stew and shepherd's pie, and the somewhat more American clam chowder. Enjoy lunch on the verandah. If you're lucky, you'll land amid an Anglican church picnic or family reunion.

Then follow Route 132 about 10km (6 miles) to Route 299, and head north through mountainous central Gaspé. Drive through forests where 200 caribou still roam. Here is **Parc de la Gaspésie**, deep in a wildlife preserve in the Chic Choc mountains, named with typical practicality by Micmac Indians who roamed these 'steep rocks' (open year round, tel: 418 763-3301 or 888 270-4483). Plan to eat dinner and stay overnight here at the **Gîte du Mont-Albert,** Route 299 (tel: 418 763-2288), where you should have booked in advance. You can camp or rent a cabin here all year round. The park's information center offers healthy choices from hiking, biking and fishing to camping and canoeing. Weather

Parc de la Gaspésie

is crucial, so consult reports on visibility. Turn back if it's rainy or foggy and don't go in September when you'll be assailed by fierce black flies. Even if it's clear, the mountain top is often cloudy, so prepare for the cold. The temperature dips to 4–5°C (approximately 40°F), as you climb.

From Mont Jacques Cartier, at 1,268m (4,160ft) the park's highest peak, you can see the St Lawrence to the north. Just after sunrise and just before sunset are the best times to spot white-tailed deer in the valley and moose in the boreal forest. To protect the caribou, access to trails on Mont Jacques Cartier is restricted to 10am to 4pm.

The road hugs the coastline

15. To the Lighthouse

This is a gentle day: a trip to a lighthouse, a leisurely lunch at Les Joyeux Naufragés in Mont St-Pierre (tel: 418 797-2017 for reservations) and a return to Gaspé by evening.

Continue on Route 299 to Ste Anne-des-Monts, where you re-join Route 132. Here the north coast turns rugged, the road jammed between the coast and the cliff. About 20km (12 miles) and twice that many curves brings you to **La Martre**'s maple-leaf red lighthouse (early June to Labor Day: daily 9am-5pm), 10 avenue de Phare. The lighthouse museum next door once housed the foghorn.

For a closer look at the zigzag cliffs and spectacular headlands, daredevils can gather at **Mont St-Pierre** for hang-gliding, para-gliding, and tandem flying. Introductory courses are run by the Centre de renseignments sur le vol libre (June 24 to August 31: daily 9am–6pm; off season, by reservation only), tel: 418 797-2222 for details.

Try **Les Joyeux Naufragés**, 7 route Pierre-Mercier in Mont-St-

The lighthouse Pierre (tel: 418 797-2017) and enjoy both views of mountain and river, along with seafood and local Québec cuisine. If time permits, continue to **L'Anse au Griffon** to visit the **Centre Socio culturel Manoir LeBoutillier**, 578 blvd Griffon (June to early September, daily 9am–7pm; September to mid-October, daily 9am–5pm; tel: 418 892-5150). This magnificent house, which dates from 1850, is a delight to explore as you learn about the life and times of the original owner, a leading cod merchant who originally hailed from the Channel Islands.

Now backtrack along Route 132 to **Rivière-au-Renard**, where Route 197 skirts Parc Forillon before re-connecting with Route 132 and returning to Gaspé.

Nunavik

One of the world's last, vast wild regions, **Nunavik** – Inuktitut for 'The Land to Live' – lures lovers of the exotic. With no major roads, few restaurants and only spartan hotels, this 500,000-sq km (193,000-sq mile) region north of the 55th parallel sees fewer than 3,000 visitors each year. If it's summer, you can maneuver a Rabaska canoe on the Rupert, sail among Ungava Bay coastal villages, raft the George, fish the Koksoak for salmon, climb the Torngat mountains, or hike in the Koroc valley. In winter, dodge drifts with snowshoes or snowmobiles, coax a dog team pulling a *qamutiik* sled, scout for wolves, camp in *igluit*, or ice-fish for char. This is a land so vast that distances are measured in parallels, not kilometers.

Before you start, consult *La Fédération des Cooperatives Nouveau-Québec* (tel: 514 457-9371/800 361-9371 from Québec, 800 465-9474 from the US) or Makivik Corporation (tel: 514 634-8091/800 361-7052), both Inuit-owned. Tourisme Québec (tel: 800 363-7777) publishes a map and brochure listing 24 travel operators, from Arctic Adventures (tel: 514 457-9371) to Wawati (tel: 819 824-7652), but makes no comment on the quality of the organizations. Adventure tours, for two persons or more,

Inuit girl

range from two days to two weeks, linking communities via speedy air safari or 10-kmh (6-mph) dogsled. If you want to come, take the advice of seasoned globetrotters: do your research and join an organized tour.

Though Nunavik represents 30 percent of Québec's land, only 10,000 people live here, including 6,800 Inuit descendants of nomads who migrated from Alaska a thousand years ago, and hold fierce ties to the land. Under the 1975 James Bay Agreement, they bargained hydroelectric development for subsidies and rights to hunting, fishing, and trapping. Makivik manages the $90 million payout.

Twin Otter fly-ins for hunting and fishing have been popular here since Robert Flaherty's film *Nanook of The North* spread romance south. From a base in **Kuujjuaq**, the region's biggest town, hunters track George River caribou, Ungava Bay walrus, and – with cameras only – the polar bear 'Lord of the Arctic.' Hunting packages have long dominated, even now representing more than 90 percent of tourism dollars. But operators, who are often bilingual, are slowly re-tooling for eco- and ethno-tourism, which emphasizes shooting photos, not animals. With this twist, you can explore Inuit culture and Arctic nature; hear throat singers in August music fests or sculpt ice figures at the snow festival at the region's first town, **Povungnituk**; wander from plain to plateau, exploring land sculpted by glaciers and stuffed with peat.

Whatever your goal – wildlife or Inuit life – prepare your pocketbook. Four nights in Kuujjuaq could cost some $1,500 – once you have paid to get there. And 10 days photographing wolves and caribou from a Cessna costs at least $4,800, including transportation. Expeditions include the services of guides, who are required

A great way to travel

for travel above the 52nd parallel. Guiding *Quallunaat* (non-Inuit people) is a strong tradition: the Inuit helped explorers hunt for the Northwest Passage and reach the Pole.

Getting to Nunavik is easy. Getting around is more difficult. You can fly direct from Montréal or Québec City to Radisson, Kuujjuarapik, and Kuujjuaq. Local carriers such as Air Inuit connect with 16 Inuit villages along Hudson and Ungava Bays, landing on gravel or tarmac. Flights depend on the weather, with frequent delays for fog in summer and hold-ups for snow in winter. Lack of competition and hefty fuel costs keep prices high. Over-booking is chronic, so check in at least an hour early, and be sure to confirm flights, reservations and airport pickups. And don't be surprised if your airport taxi is the town's truck or snowmobile.

Alternatively, you can drive 1,413km (877 miles) from Montréal to Radisson along Route 109, the world's longest private highway, a 700-km (450-mile) swathe cut across La Baie James, between parallels 49 and 55. Register at a 24-hour kiosk at Km 6 (tel: 819 739-4473 for road conditions, reservations, and registration information). Life here on Nunavik's doorstep is basic, so naturally food, warmth, and accommodation can be, too. Check out 'gas station with rooms' at Km 381.

Typical Nunavik settlement

16. A taste of Nunavik

As distances in Nunavik are so vast, this itinerary is designed to point you in the right direction rather than to be a sight-by-sight tour. Its springboard is Radisson.

Near Radisson, where Route 109 ends and Nunavik begins, you can start by exploring Hydro-Québec's huge and contentious **James Bay Hydroelectric Complex**, at **La Grande 1** or at **La Grande-2 generating station** (open all year round: daily from 1pm; tel: 800 291-8486 for reservations 48 hours in advance). Head 137m (450ft) underground. Its mega-statistics may overwhelm you, as may the sight of hilltops submerged to become islands. Fearful of more flooding and mercury pollution, the Cree people are battling Hydro-Québec's $13 billion expansion plans. To preserve the environment and the economy, these Amerindians would prefer to cater to tourists – though they have not yet matched initial Inuit tourism efforts.

About 200km (125 miles) north of Radisson, you officially cross into Nunavik, to one unique town that serves distinct residents: **Poste de la Baleine** for francophones, **Great Whale River** for anglophones, **Whapmagoostui** for Cree, and **Kuujjuarapik** for Inuit. The locals – 500 Inuit, 500 Cree, a handful of allochtones (whites) – mix at the local pool room and pub amid such boomtown streets as avenue de l'Orignal (Moose) and rue de la Tourbière (Peat Bog). Though decades of European ignorance, indifference, even racism, support the notion of cultural twins, Inuit and Cree neighbors rarely shared more than traditions as hunters and trappers. Historically, they raided each others camps for pelts and women; recently, they differed over development priorities. But both do follow wildlife and the seasons. During the summer months, Inuit families

Inuit elder

kayak to isolated shores to fish. In the fall, James Bay's 13,000 Cree abandon eight villages to manage forest traplines, often traveling by tradional canoe. Both respect the land: Inuit have seven words for ice, Cree have some 200 for woods. Both have societies under siege – hydro-development in the north and animal rights activists in the south. But both insist that they are as different as anglophones and francophones.

Away from southern influences, you will find few traditional destinations. Discovered in the 1940s, **Nouveau Québec crater** is the largest meteorite hole on earth. A near-perfect circle – 3.5km (2 miles) wide – remains from the crash 1.4 million years ago. Flights from Kangiqsujuaq buzz the 267-m (876-ft) deep lake.

If possible, spend some time in an Inuit village. Today, you're more likely to see a satellite dish than a snowhouse, and the clamor of snowmobiles has replaced the yaps of dog teams. But whether men hunt seals with well-oiled rifles or newly-sharpened harpoons, women still clean skins with a half-moon *ulu*. Don't be afraid to enter local homes or chat with village elders at the community center. These people are curious, cooperative – and quiet. You may have to offer the first *'Ullaakut'* – an Inuktitut greeting understood from Alaska to Greenland. Because Inuit still live communally, without fences or hedges marking boundaries, they tend to share what they have. Hospitality requires that you try whatever is offered, but hosts understand if you don't seek seconds. Follow their lead: sip tea when thirsty, eat 'country' food when hungry. The menu is meat, meat, and – for dessert – meat. Try caribou, raw, frozen, dried, or ground.

Vegetarian travelers should plan carefully because imports from the south are rare, with costs at least twice those in Montréal: prices are around $6 for a dozen eggs, and $25 for a chicken. At the local co-op you're likely to find candy, chips, and cookies, and alcohol may be banned. In general, the mix is healthy: high protein, vitamins, minerals. There may even be variety: bannock, seal eyes, three raw fish, a lump of seal on cardboard set on the floor. Even hotel meals may be basic: tasty Arctic char one day, and fish-sticks and fries the next .

There is also variety in weather. No one acclimatises well, so choose carefully between the region's two tourist seasons. Nunavik's winter season is late March to mid-May, summer mid-July to late August. But even the best-laid plans can ice over: Visitors tell tales of being trapped in igloos for days while 130-kph (80-mph) winds whirl outside.

The ice break-up in June signals long, bright days of spring-summer-fall. The

Igloo building

sun shines up to 17 hours a day, and the mercury soars to 15°C (59°F). But summer can still be cold, with chilling wind and rain to force you inside. Bring foil to block windows flooded with midnight sun and super-strength repellent to fend off the meddlesome black flies and mosquitoes.

Winter here is worse, with air so cold that dust freezes and people lose the ability to smell. Temperatures average -35°C (-31°F), and the darkness – there are only a few hours of twilight in December and January – may unnerve you. Fewer than 25 days a year see night-time temperatures above freezing, but proper dress can keep out most of the cold. Regardless of season, the advice is basic: layer well. In summer, bring a parka, hat, mitts, ski goggles. In winter, don't expose any skin. Outfits may cost $1,000 in Montréal, though tour companies often provide or rent clothing.

Also be prepared for disorientation. Strong wind, blinding light, pervasive silence, immense space can undermine your senses in an eery manner. Because Nunavik's landscape is monochromatic, with plains and hills covered only with snow or lichen, nothing is familiar, and you can get lost only a kilometer outside town. Maps show rivers, but compasses are unreliable so near the North Pole (at the 90th parallel). Inukshuk

Strong winds blow

rock piles to scare caribou serve only Inuit as landmarks, so don't wander alone or without giving notification.

And don't expect your hosts to entertain you. Let the streets do that! Villages with fewer than 1,000 residents are the center of Inuit life, often former Hudson's Bay Company trading posts, now transformed with government schools and clinics, plus simple aluminum pre-fab homes shipped from the south. Inside these houses you may find standards of hygiene different from your own. Be prepared to leave your shoes on a cold porch before entering a house, but don't expect to be able to take a daily bath or use crystal-clean drinking glasses.

Out in the street you might find carvers busy shaping soapstone, caribou antler, whalebone, or ivory walrus tusk, wielding traditional knives or untraditional power saws. Graphics techniques for distinctive prints are relatively new and imported from the south, where almost all craft products are marketed through co-ops that guarantee authenticity with igloo stamps. But some wonderful on-the-spot bargains are available – and they're authentic. Equally authentic are the *ennui*, the people you may find idling in some parts of town, trapped uncomfortably between ancestral traditions and contemporary anxieties.

Shopping

Québec offers non-stop, shop-to-drop opportunities. Start in **Montréal**, where you can choose from downtown **department stores**, such as Ogilvy, 1307 Ste-Catherine ouest (tel: 514 842-7711); Holt Renfrew, 1300 Sherbrooke ouest (tel: 514 842-5111), La Baie (the Hudson Bay Company, circa 1670), 585 Ste-Catherine ouest (tel: 514 281-4422); a labyrinthine underground **shopping mall**, with 29km (18 miles) of shops; elegant **arcades**, such as Les Cours Mont-Royal, 1455 Peel, or Les Promenades de la Cathédrale, 625 Ste-Catherine ouest, and prestigious shopping areas, such as **Westmount**, popular with anglophones, and **rue Laurier ouest**, popular with francophones.

Quartier Petit Champlain

Québec City abounds in interesting small shops. In the **Quartier Petit-Champlain** (just off Place-Royale in the old city's Lower Town), for instance, you will find boutiques at street level, with the appropriate workshops above. The Upper Town's **rue St Jean** is devoted to modern merchandise.

As a visitor, you may be able to claim tax rebates. Although shopping hours vary according to locale and season, stores typically open between 9 and 10am and close between 5 and 6pm weekdays, with hours extended to 8 or 9pm Thursday, Friday, and holidays. Sunday shopping is popular in the cities, though hours may be restricted. Shopkeepers are usually bilingual.

Antiques

For **antiques**, from Old World heirlooms to flea-market oddities, head for **rue St-Paul** in Québec City's Old Port, and to Old Montreal's **rue Notre-Dame**. In the **Laurentians**, look for pine Canadiana at Le Coq Rouge, 821 Ouimet, St-Jovite (tel: 819 425-3205) and in the shops that dot Route 117 in Piedmont, in particular: Antiquités Hier Pour Demain, No 914 (tel: 450 227-4231); Antiquités S Trepanier & Fils, No 670 (tel: 450 227-3532). Aux Beaux-Lauriers, 303 rue Principale St-Sauveur (tel: 450 227-3442). Specializes in accessories for antique furniture.

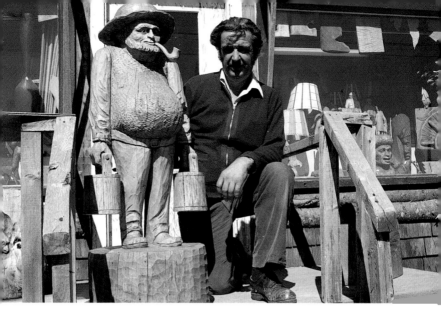

A carver with his craft

Handicrafts

In spite of the glut of plastic *camelote* (junk), you will find a good selection of **handicrafts**, from tapestry mats and quilts, to sailor chests and painted cupboards in shops and stalls all over Québec.

For a first stop in **Montréal**, try the Canadian Guild of Crafts, 2025 Peel (tel: 514 849-6091), L'Impreinte Cooperative, 272 St Paul Est (tel: 514 861-4427), Farfelu, 39 Somerville (tel: 514 488-3163); in **Québec City**, Galerie des métiers d'Art du Québec, 29 Notre Dame (tel: 418 694-0260); in **Charlevoix**, Atelier la Cire-Constance, 19 rue St-Joseph, Baie St-Paul (tel: 418 240-2473); in the **Eastern Townships**, Antiquités J–G Gélineau, 247 rue Granby, Bromont (tel: 450 534-2414); and in the **Laurentians**, galeries d'Art Claude Brocart, 2691 Curé Labelle, Prévost (tel: 450 224-4294); and the Galerie d'Art Inuit Baffin, 1514 Merette Val David, tel: 819 322-2632; and in the **Gaspé**, try Bleu Marine, Place du Quai, Percé (tel: 418 782-5302).

Fashion

It is quite easy to track down **fashion** in **Montreal**: follow banners to *la cité de la mode* or, for stylish leather, *le district de la fourrure*. For cold-climate clothes in Montreal, try Azimut, 1781 St-Denis (tel: 514 844-1717) or Kanuk, 752 St-Denis (tel: 514 527-4494), and for Québec's top designers, look for Revenge, 3852 St-Denis (tel: 514 843-4379) or Scandale, 3639 St-Laurent (tel: 514 842-4707). In the **Laurentians**, Boutique Liliane Bruneau, 2 chemin Tour de Lac, Ste-Agathe-des-Monts (tel: 819 326-1041) features more of Québec's top designers.

In the **Eastern Townships**, visit Les Versants de Bromont, at 120 blvd Bromont, which is touted as Canada's largest collection of boutique outlets (tel: 450 849-5295).

Rue du Trésor in Québec City

In the **Gaspé**, as one might expect, shops such as Les Cuirs fins de la Mer, 76 route 132 Est, Bonaventure (tel: 418 534-3821) offers clothes with a distinctly fishy theme: skirts of sole, jackets of salmon and ties of many scales. Also look out for traditional items, such as finger-woven ceinture *flechée* sashes of the type worn by Hudson's Bay Company trappers.

Art and Aboriginal works

Art galleries specializing in Québecois and Canadian artists line downtown routes in Montréal, Québec City, Baie St-Paul, and St-Sauveur. In Piedmont, visit Maison des Arts de Piedmont, 136 chemin de la Gare for exhibitions of regional artists (tel: 450 227-4322).

Aboriginal works range from Inuit graphics, engravings and soap-stone sculptures to Amerindian snowshoes, moccasins and furs, all of which make great gifts. In Québec City, you will find the best selection of aboriginal works either in shops off Place-Royale or in Old Québec. Amerindian goods and crafts can also usually be bought from the shops on Indian reservations, where more than half of Québec's Amerindians (who include many of its top craftworkers) now live.

Musées and *economusées,* small operations run by entrepreneurs along European models, also stock a wide range of goods for sale, again suitable for gifts. For example, don't miss honey made on the spot and available in candy, as well as ice cream, wine, plus inedibles, at the Musée de l'abeille, at 8862 boulevard Ste-Anne, Châtea-Richer, east of Québec City (tel: 418 824-4411).

A crafty way to advertise

Eating Out

Food – its production, preparation, and consumption – pervades *Québécois* culture. Fresh ingredients and innovative chefs ensure that eating is a day-long delight: in Québec *la gastronomie* meets *joie de vivre*.

Explore each region's cooking as well as its roads. Accredited by Québec's ministry of agriculture, some 175 members of the *Société des Chefs, Cuisiniers et Patissiers de Québec* offer delicacies ranging from tender lamb flavored by Charlevoix's seagrass, to prized *inaluaq* (seal intestines) from Nunavik and fish (fresh, pickled, smoked, and salted) landed on the Gaspé Peninsula.

Fresh salmon is a specialty

Québec's early inhabitants needed foods that could fuel long days of labor in the forest and fields, so a diet high in calories evolved. Traditional country fare includes *tourtières* (meat pies), *fèves au lard* (pork and beans), *cretons* (coarse pork *pâté*), and *tarte au sucre* (sugar pie). Québec supplies 92 percent of Canada's maple syrup; it's sold everywhere, from local grocers to souvenir shops.

Montréal and Québec City vie for having most restaurants – reputedly more than anywhere in Canada. Non-francophone immigrants to Montréal brought their own culinary treasures. In Montréal, savor **smoked meat** at Schwartz, 3895 St-Laurent (tel: 514 842-4813), and The Main, across the street at No 3864 (tel: 514 843-8126); or at the venerable Ben's, 990 de Maisonneuve ouest (tel: 514 844-1000). Also in Montreal you can munch **bagels** made 'the old way,' with honeyed water for sweetness and baked over a wood fire for heat and flavor. Queue at Fairmount Bagel Bakery, 74 Fairmount ouest (tel: 514 272-0667), or St-Viateur's Bagel, at 158 and 263 St-Viateur ouest.

Fast food has a French accent

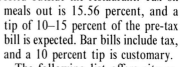

Dining out satisfies the Québécois appetite for fellowship as well as food. Perfect for people-watching and dawdling, bistros and outdoor cafés line Montréal's rue St-Denis and Québec City's Grande Allée. But even **fast food** here has a French accent, from *patates frites* sold at roadside stands to *poutine* (French fries topped with cheese curds and drenched in gravy). Try **St-Hubert Bar BQ** for chicken, or **Pizzèdélic** or **Pizzaiolle** for 'you-ate-it-here-first' combos. Alternatively order a dog 'all dressed' (the usual plus shredded cabbage and cayenne pepper).

In Montréal, eating starts early and continues until late, especially at such round the clock spots as **Club Sandwich**, 1570 Sainte-Catherine est (tel: 523-4679). In the country, hours are much more limited, with restaurants, inns, and auberges usually open noon–3pm and then 5.30–9pm.

Whether you are enjoying *haute cuisine* in an elegant resort or tucking into the cheap and cheerful fare of a backroom bistro, you will find food cooked and served with flair. Because the Québecois consider themselves connoisseurs not only of food but of service, atmosphere and setting, only exceptional restaurants survive. Even without looking far afield, you will find *honnête* (good-value) food which is fresh and filling.

A few practical tips before feasting: some restaurants allow you to bring your own wine, so call ahead. Buy wine or spirits in the *Société des Alcools* stores run by the province, which are cheaper and better stocked than the local *dépanneur* (convenience store). You must be 18 to buy or drink liquor. If you're on a tight budget, look for good-value midday specials. Even in the evening, many restaurants will offer a *table d'hôte* (set menu) at an affordable price. By law, prices must be posted outside the restaurant. Tax on meals out is 15.56 percent, and a tip of 10–15 percent of the pre-tax bill is expected. Bar bills include tax, and a 10 percent tip is customary.

The following list offers city establishments only. Ideas for eating out in other towns and areas are contained in the itineraries section of this guide. Prices in the following list are based on a meal for one, excluding tax, tip and wine, and are in Canadian dollars.

$ = under $10
$$ = $10–$20
$$$ = $20–$30
$$$$ = $30–plus

Harvest feast

Lunch

Québec City

L'ÉCHAUDÉ
73 rue du Sault-au-Matelot
Tel: 418 692-1299
French gourmet. $$

LE PARIS-BREST
590 Grande Allée
Tel: 418 529-2243
French cooking in noisy basement. $$

Montréal

BIO TRAIN
410 rue St-Jacques ouest
Tel: 514 842-9184
Popular self-serve health food. $

LE COMMENSAL
1204 avenue McGill College
Tel: 514 871-1480
2115 St-Denis
Tel: 514 845-2627
Veggie buffet and desserts to go. $$

SANTROPOL
3990 rue St Urbain
Tel: 514 842-3110
Salads and huge sandwiches. $$

Dinner

Québec City

A LA TABLE DE SERGE BRUYÈRE
1200 rue St Jean
Tel: 418 694-0618
Nouvelle cuisine. $$$$

AUX ANCIENS CANADIENS
34 rue St-Louis
Tel: 418 692-1627
Well-known *habitant* food. $$$

L'ASTRAL
Hôtel Loews Le Concorde
1225 Place Montcalm
Tel: 418 647-2222
Panoramic view, gourmet food. $$$

Montréal

THE BEAVER CLUB
Hôtel la Reine Elizabeth
900 Boulevard René Lévesque ouest
Tel: 514 861-3511
Classical *haute cuisine* served in a dining room decked with beaver furs and trophies. $$$

GIBBYS
298 Place d'Youville
Tel: 514 282-1837
This 200-year-old stables adorned with antiques is the place to go for huge steaks. $$$

Decisions, decisions

LES HALLES
1450 rue Crescent
Tel: 514 844-2328
Fabulous French food served in Parisian style. $$$$

LALOUX
250 avenue des Pins e.
Tel: 514 287-9127
A Nineties decor and wonderful French food. One 'must' is the foie gras, regardless of cost! $$$

STEAK FRITES
12 rue St-Paul est
Tel: 514 842-0972
Steak and French fries served in a multitude of ways. $

Nightlife

Nightlife in Québec depends on where you are. Montréal and Québec City have theaters, cinemas, restaurants, bistros, and bars, and late-night partying here usually starts late and ends just before dawn. Outside the big cities, you will find village pubs and summer theater that draw 'locals' from miles around.

Even in the winter months few people simply cozy up to VCRs, because this is when hockey, the national passion, takes over. At the Molson Centre, a new stadium at 1250 rue de la Gauchetière

Ice-hockey is a passion

ouest, you can see the **Canadiens**. Seats for the 40 home games played between October and June are hard to come by, so reserve early (tel: 514 932-2582).

Québec City's beloved hockey team, the Nordiques, moved to the US. However, a professional baseball team, Les Capitales, had a successful inaugural season in 1999 at Québec City's municipal stadium, 100 rue du Cardinal Maurice-Roy (tel: 418 521-2255). Tickets are priced modestly – from $5 to $12.

Less exalted but still beloved are the **Expos**, Montréal's National League baseball team. Pick from 80 home games played between April and September, at Olympic Stadium, 4549 Pierre-de-Coubertin (tel: 514 790-1245 or www.montrealexpos.com).

Those who prefer highbrow entertainment can listen to orchestras and operas at Montréal's **Place des Arts**, 175 rue Ste-Catherine ouest (tel: 514 790-ARTS or 800-203-ARTS), and Québec City's **Capitole Theatre**, 972 rue St-Jean (tel: 418 694-4444). Visitors of all tastes will enjoy performances by **Cirque du Soleil**, former street performers from Baie-St-Paul who now captivate audiences worldwide with their three-hour stints of amazing acrobatics. Track these *artistes* to Montreal where they launch new programmes, 1217 Notre Dame est (tel: 514 522-2324).

Meanwhile anyone over the age of 18 who enjoys a flutter can visit the **Casino de Montréal** (tel: 392-2746/800 665-2274), on

Dance at Place des Arts

Ile Nôtre-Dame. This state-of-the-art casino was so packed in its first year that officials decided to double its size. They also opened a second casino at Pointe au Pic's **Manoir Richelieu** (tel: 800 665-2274). For other nightspots in Montréal, explore **boulevard St-Laurent** and **rue St-Denis**. Montréal keeps later hours than the rest of Québec, with clubbers looking for post-party snacks at 3am. Students favor Montréal's **rue St-Denis**, south of rue Sherbrooke.

In Québec City, investigate the **Grande Allée** or around **La Gare du Palais**, the city's revitalized train station near *Le Vieux Port*. University students tend to cluster at **Quartier Latin** cafés along **rue Couillard**.

An enjoyable way to spend an evening in either city, especially if it's warm, is to eat dinner aboard a *Bâteau Mouche* cruising from Montréal (tel: 514 849-9952) or a Croisières AML cruise from Québec city's old port (tel: 418 692-1159).

Outside the cities, follow locals to nightlife landmarks. In **Charlevoix**, for example, Domaine Forget outside Ste-Irénée hosts summer concerts, classical and jazz, from mid-June to late-August (tel: 418 452-3535 or 1 888-336-7438).

In the **Laurentians**, St-Sauveur, Ste-Adèle and Ste-Agathe have no shortage of bars, bistros, outdoor cafés, indoor discos, and *après-ski* entertainment on offer.

Montréal is good for jazz

Calendar of Special Events

Québecers celebrate their province each summer with more than 200 festivals. They seize any excuse for an outing – potatoes, jazz, film, lobsters, and even snow. *Fêtes* in Montréal and Québec City may be more sophisticated, but not necessarily more fun than those in the countryside, as Eastern Townshippers at the Big Brome Fair will attest. Most outdoor festivals are free – once you have payed for the picnic and cold beer.

Winters don't keep Québecers inside. A tradition dating from the 1880s, winter *carnavals*, draw visitors worldwide. For more information about festivals in Québec, contact Société des Fêtes et Festivals du Québec (tel: 514 252-3037 or 800 361-7688).

Carnival mascot

JANUARY / FEBRUARY

In mid-February, Québec City's **Winter Carnival**/Carnaval d'Hiver, held every year since 1954, offers 10 days of icy delights, including snow palaces, canoe races, and ice sculpting, and 10 nights of parades, masquerade balls, firework displays, midnight bars, and buffets. Some aspects of the Carnaval d'Hiver never change, including the cheery snowman mascot, *Bonhomme Carnaval*, and the *carnavaleux* dancers (tel: 418 626-3716).

In early February, the **Montreal Snow Festival**/Fête des Neiges takes the chill out of winter, filling Parc des Iles with snow castles and ice slides. You can compete against locals in kite-skating, barrel-jumping, and dog sled- or ice canoe-racing (tel: 514 872-4537 for details).

MARCH / APRIL

Maple-mania is a rite of spring throughout rural Québec, especially in **'sugaring off festivals'** held throughout the Laurentians and Eastern Townships. At *cabanes à sucre* (sugar shacks), pancakes sizzle, beans bubble, pork rinds crackle, and maple syrup chills on snow. Follow the local example and try drinking sap straight from the pail, bugs and all.

Children at a winter carnival in the Laurentians

MAY / JUNE

In mid-June, cover your ears at Canada's only world circuit of Formula One racing, on Montreal's Ile Nôtre-Dame. Drivers compete for three days at the Grand Prix Air Canada on the 4.4-km (2¾-mile) Gilles Villeneuve track (tel: 514 350-0000 for further details).

From early June through July, pyrotechnic experts from a dozen countries blast fireworks over Montreal during eight consecutive weekends in the Benson & Hedges Inc **International Fireworks Competition**. Shows begin after dusk, usually at 10pm, at La Ronde amusement park on Ile Ste-Hélène (tel: 514 872-4537 for details).

One day each June, some 45,000 brave cyclists pedal a 65-km (40-mile) route in the Montréal Bike Fest/Tour de l'Ile de Montréal. The route taken varies – sometimes it runs inside the city limits and sometimes it heads outside of them (tel: 514 521-8536 for further information).

June 24 is **St-Jean-Baptiste Day/** Fête Nationale du Québec. Popular festivities signal summer, and illustrated T-shirts depict frogs kicking beavers.

JULY / AUGUST

July 1 is Canada Day, honoring Confederation with air shows, parades, concerts, and a rash of picture T-shirts, this time depicting beavers kicking frogs (tel: 514 866-9164).

Early to mid-July, jazz and blues performers from all over the world converge on Montréal for 10 days filled with 350 concerts at the **International Jazz Festival/**Festival International de Jazz. Big-name performers pack large venues as well as the city's more intimate clubs, but others perform outdoors for free. Hit the streets, along

Pyrotechnics

At the Just for Laughs festival

with a million other visitors (tel: 514 871-1881 or 888 515-0515).

There's more music to be heard, this time classical, at **Festival Orford**, in which performances by the Jeunesses Musicales du Canada draw a wealth of talent to the Eastern Townships (tel: 819 843-3981 or 800 567-6155).

For 10 days in early July, the **du Maurier Québec Summer Festival**/Festival d'Eté de Québec du Maurier turns over streets and squares in Vieux-Québec to more than 1,000 performers in some 400 shows. You can expect to find humor (from clowns to comedians), food (from popcorn to *pâté*), and music (punk to Puccini). Tel: 418 692-4540 or 888 992-5200 for details.

From mid-July to early August each year, Montreal hosts the **Just for Laughs Festival**/Festival Juste Pour Rire. During 10 full days of fun, nearly 500 acrobats, street comedians, mime artists, clowns, and jokesters stage up to 300 shows in the world's largest bilingual comedy festival. Tel: 514 790-4242 (790-HAHA) for further details. (For laughs at other times of the year, you can always step inside the Just for Laughs Museum/Musée Juste Pour Rire, at 2111 Boulevard St-Laurent, Montréal.)

AUGUST / SEPTEMBER

Performance artists from around the world offer French songs and skits at Les Francofolies de Montréal, which takes place for 10 days in early August (tel: 514 525-7732).

From late August until early September, film-makers and film watchers spend 10 days at The **Montréal World Film Festival**/Festival des Films du Monde. You can flit between a half dozen downtown cinemas and 250 movies, from shorts to feature-length (tel: 514 848-3883).

SEPTEMBER / OCTOBER

For 10 days in mid-September each odd-numbered year, the **International Festival of New Dance**/Festival International de Nouvelle Danse in Montréal features dance from around the world (tel: 514 287-1423).

Film-makers out of the mainstream head to Montreal for the **International New Cinema and Video Festival**/ Festival International du Nouveau Cinéma et de la Vidéo de Montréal, which shows a selection of Third World and non-traditional films for 10 days each October (tel: 514 843-4725).

Autumn is celebrated in the 10-day **Autumn Dreams**/Rêves d'automne festival in Baie-St-Paul in late September and early October, with art exhibits, workshops, mountain climbing and biking. Artists open studios and lead workshops (tel: 800 761-5150).

NOVEMBER / DECEMBER

Celebrations peter out as winter takes hold. However, the festive spirit revives over the Christmas period.

PRACTICAL information

GETTING THERE

Getting to Québec is easy. Rails and roads are well-maintained, and more than 40 airlines frequent Montréal's airports. Regional airlines serve smaller cities, and bush planes connect villages in the north.

By air: Dorval airport handles domestic, US and international flights, and Mirabel domestic and international charter flights (tel: 514 394-7377 or 800 465-1213 for both airports). Dorval is about 22km (14 miles), or half an hour's drive from downtown Montréal, while Mirabel is 55km (34 miles), or 45 minutes from the center. Flights are also frequent between Dorval and Ste-Foy airport, about 20 minutes from downtown Québec City.

Take to the road

By bus: Montréal Central Bus Station serves all long-distance routes (Berri-UQAM Metro station), 505 de Maisonneuve est (tel: 514 843-4231). Québec City's terminal is at 320 rue Abraham-Martin (tel: 418 525-3000). Grayline de Québec (tel: 418 523-9722) offers 14-day unlimited travel fares from May until late October.

By road: More than 20,000km (12,500 miles) of roads criss-cross the province, though no highways penetrate the north. Speed limits – 50kmh (30mph) in cities, 80kmh (50mph) on two-lane highways, and 100kmh (60mph) on freeways – are enforced. Fasten your seatbelt, and leave your radar detector at home.

By train: Amtrak (tel: 800 872-7245) and Via Rail (tel: 1-888-VIA-RAIL) trains arrive in Montréal at the Central Station (Bonaventure Metro station), 935 de la Gauchetière ouest, which links regional and commuter trains. Gare-du-Palais, 450 rue de la Gare du Palais, serves Québec City trains (tel: 418 524-4161). A Canrail pass allows discounts for Via Rail travel on any 12 days in a 30-day period.

TRAVEL ESSENTIALS

Visas / Passports / Customs

To enter Canada from any country but the United States, you must have a valid passport and may need a visa. US citizens or permanent residents need only official identification such as a driver's license. Visitors staying longer than three months may need a visa.

Border formalities are usually simple and fast, providing you leave your handguns or automatic weapons at home. For details, contact Ministère des Affaires Extérieures du Canada (tel: 514 283-2152).

GETTING ACQUAINTED

Population/Geography

Twice the size of both Texas and France, Québec covers a massive 1,540,000 sq km (595,000 sq miles), stretching from midcontinent to the Atlantic, and from the US border to the Hudson Strait. About 85 percent of the land mass is untamed. Some 3,000 rivers and more than half a million lakes – only 10 percent of them with names – dot the landscape.

More than half of Québec's 6 million residents live in or near Montréal. Canada's largest city after Toronto, Montréal has 1,700,000 city residents, with another 3,300,000 in Greater Montréal. More than 630,000 people live in or near the provincial capital, Québec City.

Three of Québec's 6 million residents

Weights and Measures

Canada operates on the metric system. Multiply kilometers by 0.621371 to get miles. If that sounds complicated, simply divide by eight and multiply by five. To convert Celsius into Fahrenheit, divide the Celsius temperature by 5, multiply by 9 and add 32. For Celsius, subtract 32 from the Fahrenheit reading, divide by 9 and multiply by 5. There are 3.8 liters in 1 US gallon.

Time

Québec follows Eastern Standard Time.

Electricity

Electrical current is 110 volts, 60 cycles, alternating current. Appliances from the US do not need converters; those from Europe do.

Weather

Québec's climate is continental. Spring and fall are cool and damp; summers and winters, extreme. Temperatures in Montréal average -9.5°C (16°F) in January and 21°C (70°F) in July. For the province, they average -11.6°C(-11F) in January and 16.3°C (61.3°F) in June. Rainfall averages 78cm (31in), with annual snowfall exceeding 242cm (95in).

For weather forecasts in Montréal, tel: 514 283-4006 (English). For forecasts in Québec City, tel: 418 648-7766.

Winter

French author Voltaire snubbed French Canada as 'so many useless acres of snow not worth fighting over with the British,' and *Québécois* singer Gilles Vigneault conceded, albeit with love: 'My land is not a land, it is winter.' The season is traditionally mid-November to mid-April, but temperatures may dip below freezing in early November, and snow may hang on until May.

But winter is not boring. One in three households possesses cross-country skis, one in four downhill skis – the highest proportion in the world. With November's first snow, head for the 26,700km (16,600 miles) of ski trails: well-marked, well-maintained, well-chilled.

The province has two mountain ranges that tally more than 300cm (130in) of snow annually. Low mountains, and snow machines, guarantee solid if not spectacular skiing. From Montréal, head to the Laurentians or the Eastern Townships. From Québec City, drive about 30 minutes to Stoneham (tel: 418 848-2411 or 800 463-6888) or Mont Ste-Anne (tel: 418 827-4561 or 888 827-4579).

Slopes, chairlifts, and towlines can become extremely crowded on weekends and holidays, with ski-boarders competing for space, so go during the week if you can. You can ski by the hour, by the run, or by the season.

Waiting for spring

For a more sedentary thrill, climb aboard a snowmobile, with registration, insurance, and a pass, to carry you on the 26,000-km (16,150-mile) network of trails, including 9,000km (5,590 miles) in the Trans-Québec network. Trails are often old railway lines or logging roads with heated shelters and regular patrols. Or try other winter treats, many unique: dogsledding, snowshoeing, ice fishing, or skate sailing. Montréal also has some 200 ice rinks.

MONEY MATTERS

Currency Exchange

Visitors may exchange currency at all major banks and at foreign exchange dealers, with no restrictions on amounts. Rates at banks are generally better. Common bills – $5, $10, $20, $50, $100 – vary in color. Look for coins with moose, beavers, loons (on the $1 coin known as a 'loonie'), and bears on the new silver and brass $2 coin. In tourist areas, other currencies, especially US dollars, are accepted, though not at the best rate. The prices given in this guide refer to Canadian, not American, dollars.

Tipping

Coat checkers, doormen and porters expect $1 per item. Waiters, waitresses, and taxi drivers expect 10–15 percent of the pre-

tax total. Some restaurants may add an automatic service charge for groups.

Tax relief

A 7 percent federal tax (GST/TPS) is applied to most goods and services throughout Canada. A provincial tax (PST/TVQ) of 6.5 percent is also added to all goods and services.

Be sure to apply for a GST/TPS rebate on short-term accommodations and goods bought for use outside Canada. The form 'GST rebate for visitors' is available from Revenue Canada's Ottawa office and most tourist shops. You can claim rebates up to $500 in person at duty-free shops at borders and airports. For a larger rebate, apply by mail.

Applications must include bills of sale or itemized receipts. Accommodation receipts must show the number of nights of lodging supplied. For visitor rebates, tel: 800-668-4748. For rebates on the provincial sales tax, tel: 514 873-4692.

Some traders may offer to pay sales taxes as a bid for business. Others will offer discounts for cash deals, which feed the underground economy rather than the revenue collectors.

GETTING AROUND

Private cars

Although the most practical way to see far-flung Québec is by car, driving here can be tricky. Traffic signs are unilingually French. Some pictograms are highly-developed, others obscure.

Drivers and passengers must wear seatbelts. While pedestrians have the right of way at crosswalks, drivers usually ignore this. Bus drivers have the right of way, and they use it.

Montréal has two distinct seasons on the roads: winter and road repair. (For summer construction reports, contact Info Route, tel: 514 873-4121; for winter weather conditions, contact Environment Canada, tel: 514 283-3010)

In towns and cities, parking signs are complex and tricky, and fines are steep, with the cost of towing topping the penalty (tel: 514 280-4636 during work hours – 911 at other times – if you think your

car has been towed away). The scene in Québec City, is equally atrocious: public parking lots, marked by large Ps, fill up early, leaving late sleepers to circle and circle, growing increasingly frustrated in their search for a space.

If you are bringing a car into Québec, you must also bring a valid driver's license, vehicle registration documents, and liability insurance (which covers damage to someone else's property or person) for a minimum of $50,000.

Rental Cars

Most car rentals have branches at the airports and in major hotels as well as central offices downtown. The following agencies may have several locations in Montréal, including at both airports: Alamo Rent-A-Car (tel: 514 633-1222 or 800-327-9633); Thrifty (tel: 514 631-0599 or 800-367 2277); Hertz (tel: 514 631-7035 or 800 263-0600); National Tilden (tel: 878-2771 or 800 387 4747); Discount (tel: 514 286-1554 or 800 263-2355).

In Québec City try Avis (tel: 418 872-2861); Via Route (tel: 418 682-2660); National Tilden (tel: 418 871-1224).

Emergency road service

Contact Canadian Automobile Association CAA-Québec (in Montréal, tel: 514 861-7111 or 800 336-HELP; in Québec City, tel: 418 624-0708; emergency tel: 418 624-4000.

Car Pool

For a ride-sharing service operating a car pool from Montréal to the US, Québec City, Toronto, Ottawa, contact Allostop, tel: 514 985-3032 or 418 522-0056.

Taxis

In Montréal, taxi rates are fixed at $3.00 to start plus $1 per extra kilometer. Try Taxi Veteran, tel: 514 273-6351; Taxi Diamond, tel: 514 273-6331; Taxi La Salle, tel: 514 277-2552.

In Québec City: Taxi Coop, tel: 418 525-5191; Taxi Québec: tel: 418 525-8123.

Bicycle Rentals

Cyclists can use municipal paths or regional trails overseen by Vélo Québec. For maps and guides, tel: 514 521-8356.

In Montréal, rent bikes at la Maison des cyclistes, tel: 514 521-8356; Quadricycle International Inc, tel: 514 849-9953; Vélo Aventure Montréal, tel: 514 847-0666.

Public Transit

Public transportation in Montréal, Québec City and Hull is both efficient and inexpensive. Montréal has an excellent Metro and bus service. To plot your Montréal route, call Autobus (tel: 514 288-6287). Ensure you have the exact change for the bus. Monthly, three-day and one-day passes, and a strip of six tickets are available at discount. Transfer tickets are valid for 90 minutes.

Ferries cross the St Lawrence from St-Siméon to Rivière du Loup, crossing time 65–90 minutes (tel: 418 638-2856).

River ferry

Business hours

Shops are generally open Monday to Wednesday 10am–6pm, 9pm on Thursday and Friday. Saturday 10am–5pm. Some city stores are open on Sunday. In tourist areas, shopkeepers keep flexible hours. Museums follow regular business hours, but close Monday or Tuesday.

Public holidays

New Year's Day: January 1
January 2 (unofficial, but most businesses and government offices are closed)
Good Friday: date varies
Easter Monday: date varies
Fête de Dollard (formerly Victoria Day), is the second from last Monday in May
Le Fête Nationale (St-Jean Baptiste Day): June 24
Canada Day: July 1
Labor Day: first Monday in September
Thanksgiving Day: the second Monday in October
Remembrance Day: November 11 (holiday for banks and federal agencies, but not for stores and provincial agencies)
Christmas Day: December 25
Boxing Day: December 26

ACCOMMODATION

Tourisme Québec offers a reservation service for 400 establishments in the province and will be able to advise you on establishments offering the type of accommodation you require (tel: 800 363-7777 or 800 482-2433).

The Infotouriste organization will help you find rooms both in Montréal (tel: 514 873-2015/800 363-7777) and in Québec City (tel: 418 694-2608).

For youth hostel information, call Tourisme Jeunesse (tel: 514 252-3117).

Prices peak in high season (May to October), but special rates and discounts are often available and some hoteliers may be willing to negotiate room rates. The current daily average rate in Montréal is $90–$100. Always make reservations in advance and confirm rates when you make the booking.

Lodgings outside cities range from all-year-round resorts to smaller hotels and family-run inns. Condominiums, chalets, and B&Bs are also available. Note that in ski resorts, weeks always begin on Sunday night.

In the following list of recommended hotels, $$$ = over $200 a night for a double room; $$ = $100–$200; $ = under $100 (all based on Canadian dollars). Bed and Breakfasts usually fall between the two latter categories (*see page 84*).

Montréal

AUBERGE DE LA FONTAINE
1301 Rachel est
Tel: 514 597-0166 or 800 597-0597
www.aubergedelafontaine.com
Turreted greystone triplex offer rooms with views, parking, kitchen, and breakfast. **$$**

AUBERGE DE JEUNESSE INTERNATIONAL
Youth Hostel, 1030 Mackay
Tel: 514 843-3317
Dormitories and private rooms. **$**

Le Chateau Versailles

LE CHATEAU VERSAILLES
1659 Sherbrooke ouest
Tel: 514 933-3611, 800 361-7199 (Canada), 800 361-3664 (US)
www.tourversailles.com
Comprising four stately Edwardian stone townhouses located near downtown sites. **$$$**

HILTON MONTREAL BONAVENTURE
1 Place Bonaventure
Tel: 514 878-2332, 800-HILTONS
www.hilton.com
Central location with gloriously peaceful rooftop gardens. **$$$**

HOTEL DE L'INSTITUT
3535 rue St-Denis
Tel: 514 282-5120 or 800 361-5111 (Québec)
e-mail: hotel@ithq.qc.ca
This hotel offers value and service. Reserve well in advance. **$$**

MCGILL UNIVERSITY RESIDENCES
3935 University
Tel: 514 398-6367
From mid-May to mid-August, you can rent a spartan room in a grand location for $27–33 a night. Reserve early. **$**

RITZ-CARLTON MONTREAL
1228 Sherbrooke ouest
Tel: 514 842-4212, 800 363-0366
www.ritzcarlton.com
Unbeatable location and service. **$$$**

DOWNTOWN YMCA
1450 Stanley
Tel: 514 849-8393
Near Rue Sherbrooke. Most rooms are available with shared facilities. **$**

YWCA DE MONTRÉAL
1355 René Lévesque ouest
Tel: 514 866-9941
Near rue Crescent, some rooms are available with semi-private baths. **$**

Welcome to your B&B

Bed & Breakfasts

The following networks represent over 50 homes in the city, and others across the province. Prices range between $45–55 for a single, $65–90 for a double. Outside the cities, lodging may be seasonal, so reserve ahead.

A DOWNTOWN (MTL) NETWORK
Tel: 514 289-9749/800 267-5180
BED AND BREAKFAST CITY-WIDE NETWORK
Tel: 514 738-9410/800 738-4338
RELAIS MONTREAL HOSPITALITE
Tel: 514 287-9635/800 363-9635
BED & BREAKFAST BIENVENUE
Tel: 514 844-5897/800 227-5897

Québec City

AUBERGE ST-ANTOINE
10 rue St-Antoine
Tel: 418 692-2211/888 692-2211
www.saint-antoine.com

A magnificently restored maritime warehouse in the Lower Town. **$$**

LE CHATEAU FRONTENAC
1 des Carrières
Tel: 418 692-3861/800 441-1414
www.cphotels.ca
Grand lodgings in 610 grand rooms. **$$$**

HOTEL DOMINION 1912
126 rue St-Pierre
Tel: 418 692-2224/888 833-5253
www.hoteldominion.com
Close to Place Bonaventure, this 9-storey former office tower was the city's first skyscraper. Luxurious rooms, great location. **$$**

HOTEL LA MAISON DEMERS
68 rue Ste-Ursule
Tel: 418 692-2487
This delightful B&B has been going for over 30 years. **$–$$**

HOTEL MANOIR D'AUTEUIL
49 rue d'Auteuil
Tel: 418 694-1173
This 1835 house has 16 Art Deco-style rooms. Continental breakfast. **$$–$$$**

Laurentians
AUBERGE DU LAC-DES-SABLES
230 rue St-Venant
Ste-Agathe-des-Montes
Tel: 819 326-3994/800 567-8329
www.aubergedulac.com
Tranquil rooms beside a tranquil lake. **$$**

AUBERGE LE ST-VENANT
234 rue St-Venant
Ste-Agathe-des-Monts
Tel: 819 326-7937/800 679-7937
www.venant6int/laurentides.qc.ca
This serene B&B has a pleasant deck which offers inviting views. **$$**

Charlevoix
AUBERGE DES FALAISES
18 chemin des Falaises
Pointe au Pic
Tel: 418 665-3731/800 386-3731
www.aubergedesfalaises.com
De-luxe accommodations in 12 rooms and a new 32-room pavilion. Wonderful *nouvelle cuisine*. **$$**

AUBERGE LA ROMANCE
129 chemin des Falaises
Pointe au Pic
Tel: 418 665-4865
www.quebecweb.com/laromance
Pretty, distinctive rooms. $$–$$$

LE MANOIR RICHELIEU
181 rue Richelieu
Pointe au Pic
Tel: 418 665-3703/800 441-1414
www.cphotels.ca
A 400-room stone castle,with a golf course, tennis courts, a pool, and a casino. $$

Cantons de l'Est(Eastern Townships)

AUBERGE DU JOLI VENT
667 chemin Bondville
Lac Brome/Foster
Tel: 450 243-4272
Charming old family-run inn, renowned for its cooking. $

CEDAR GABLES
4080 rue Magog
North Hatley
Tel: 819 842-4120
This comfortable 1890 home offers private baths, plus lakeside breakfasts. $–$$

MANOIR HOVEY
Chemin Hovey
North Hatley
Tel: 819 842-2421, 800 661-2421
www.manoirhovey.com
Grand setting, with cuisine to match. $$$

MOTEL CYPRES
592 Lakeside
Lac Brome/Knowlton
Tel: 514 243-0363
Lake views and individual kitchenettes. $

Gaspé

AUBERGE DU GARGANTUA
222 Route des Failles
Percé
Tel: 418 782-2852
Good base for the peninsula, comfortable rooms, plus campground. $–$$

GITE BAIE JOLIE
270 Montée Wakeham
Gaspé

Tel: 418 368-2149
Comfortable rooms but no private baths. $

GITE DU MONT-ALBERT
Sainte-Anne-des-Monts
Tel: 418 763-2288/888-270-4483
Quiet rooms in the heart of the Parc de la Gaspésie. $

GITE LA NORMANDE
19 rue Davis, Gaspé
Tel: 418 368-5468
www.gites-classifies.qc.ca/norm.htm
With a pool but no private baths. $

The elegant Manoir Hovey

HOTEL LA NORMANDIE
221 Route 132 Ouest
Percé
Tel: 418 782-2112 or 800 463-0820
Elegant white clapboard offering great hospitality and *haute cuisine*. $–$$

MOTEL ADAMS
20 rue Adams
Gaspé
Tel: 418 368-2244, 800 463-4242
Large, welcoming hotel-motel. $

RIOTEL PERCE
10 rue de l'Auberge
Percé
Tel: 418 782-5535/888 427-7374
www.riotel.qc.ca
Year-round snowmobile stopover. 12 motel complexes. $

Camping

Campgrounds are voluntarily rated for service and facilities by the Camping

Québec (tel: 450 651-7396/1-800-363-0457) or www.campingquebec.com.

Québec's 20 national and provincial parks offer accommodations ranging from wilderness campsites to cabins large enough for a dozen people. Private inns and hotels are often located nearby. For information on provincial parks, contact the Ministère du Loisir, de la Chasse et de la Pêche du Québec; for national park information, tel: 800 463-6769 from Canada or 418 648-4177.

EMERGENCIES

For emergencies in and near Montréal (police, fire, ambulance) dial 911. Elsewhere, dial 0. For items lost on Montréal public transport, tel: 514 280-4637. If you leave property in a Montréal taxi, tel: 514 273-1725.

COMMUNICATION AND MEDIA

Telephones

Québec has four area codes. Montréal and environs: 514; Montréal's surrounding areas: 450; Québec City, the Gaspé and eastern Québec: 418; Eastern Townships, Hull, and northern Québec: 819. To call Canada, dial 1, then the area code and telephone number. For overseas calls, dial 0. Operators speak French and English.

Newspapers

Two free English-language tabloids, *The Mirror* and *Hour*, and a French-language counterpart, *Voir*, are published weekly in Montréal. They list night clubs, restaurants, and other entertainment venues.

For French newspapers in Montréal, choose among these dailies: *La Presse* or *Le Journal de Montréal*; *Le Devoir* for the intelligentsia, or *Allo Police* for the not-so-intelligentsia. In Québec City, look for dailies *Le Soleil*, *Journal de Québec*, or a monthly magazine *Voilà Québec*. Québec's main English-language papers are Montréal's daily *The Gazette* and Québec City's weekly *The Chronicle Telegraph*.

Post

Post offices are generally open from 8am–5pm, Monday to Friday, but closed

Here comes the mail

on Saturday. However, a number of retail outlets have a postal counter that is open on Saturday and Sunday.

TOURS

Montréal

Tours are offered in French and English. Packages range from $20–50, according to duration, content, and distance. Call for details. Many run only May through October. For tickets and departure points in Montréal, head to Infotouriste, 1001 Dorchester Square.

By bus
Autocar Connaisseur Gray Line, tel: 514 934-1222
Montréal Sightseeing, tel: 514 484-0104
Step On Guides, tel: 514 935-5131
Autocar Royal Tour de Ville, tel: 514 871 4733
L'autre Montréal Tours (a non-profit organization operating in major ethnic neighbourhoods), tel: 514 521-7802

By foot
Old Montréal Ghost Train conducts walking tours that take participants back to the days of the French colony. For details tel: 514 863-0303. In summer, guided walking or motor tours visit various Montréal churches to see the stained glass windows of **Guido Nincheri**, tel: 514 256-4636. Kéroul, tel: 514 252-3104, provides information

on accessible Montréal for people with restricted physical ability.

By boat
Bâteau mouche, tel: 514 849-9952
Harbour cruises, tel: 514 842-3871
Lachine Rapids tour, tel: 514 284-9607
Rafting on the St Lawrence, tel: 767-2230
Amphitour, tel: 514 933-6674

Québec City

By bus/trolley
Gray Line, tel: 418 653-9722
Maple Leaf Step-On Guide (a narrated, 90-minute city tour, allowing you to re-board free at 12 scheduled stops, which runs from 8.30am–3.30pm during the summer), tel: 418 622-3677
Old Québec Tours, tel: 418 664-0460
Les Tours historiques de Québec, tel: 418 872-2838

By foot
Maple Leaf Step-on Service (mid-June to early July 10am–1pm) tel: 418 622-3677
Contact Québec, tel: 418 692 2801
Les Tours Adlard, tel: 418 692 2358

By boat
Catamaran Famille Dufour II, tel: 418 827-5711; 800 463-5250
Croisières AML Cruises, tel: 418 692-1150; 800 563-4643
M/V Le Coudrier II, tel: 418 692-0107

Charlevoix

Croisière Express, tel: 418 235-4770
Croisières AML, tel: 418 237-4272 or 800-463-1292
Hotel Tadoussac Cruiser (from $40), tel: 418 235-4421

![LANGUAGE]

For the greater part – more than 80 percent – of all Québecers, French is still *la langue maternelle* – the mother tongue. By provincial law, although not by federal law, French is the sole language of government and business.

Francophone *Québécois* are proud of their linguistic heritage, even though citizens of France point out differences. His-

torical ties to Britain and America mean that Québec's French is laced with anglicizations, although the *Office de la Langue Française* insist on *la fin de semaine* (not *le weekend*) and disavow *joual* (Montréal's earthy street dialect) as incorrect grammatically, if not politically.

Many residents speak 'Frenglish,' a unique Québec mix, which is recognized as distinct in the *Oxford Companion to the English Language*. Here, English speakers consume *frites*, bank at the *caisse pop-*

Fishing trips

ulaire, and seek government *subventions* rather than grants.

Many Montréalers are bilingual, even trilingual; elsewhere in the province, however, bilingualism is more a rumor than a reality.

![USEFUL ADDRESSES]

Tourist Offices:
Centre Infotouriste, 1001 Square Dorchester, Montréal. June 1 to Labor Day: 7am–8pm; rest of the year 9am– 6pm; tel: 873-2015 or 800 363-7777.
Tourisme Montréal, 1555 Peel, Montréal, tel: 514 844-5400.
Greater Québec Area Tourism and Convention Bureau, 835 avenue Wilfrid-Laurier, Québec City, tel: 418 649-2608, 800 363-7777 (US and Canada).

Laurentian Tourist Association, tel: 450 436-8532 or 800 561-6673; website: www.laurentides.com
Gaspé Tourist Association, tel: 418 775-2223 or 800 463-0323; website: www.tourisme-gaspesie.com
Charlevoix Tourist Association, tel: 418 665-4454 or 800-667 2276; website: www.tourisme-charlevoix.com
Eastern Townships Tourist Association, tel: 819 820-2020 and 800-355 5755; website: www.tourisme-cantons.qc.ca
Nunavik/FCNQ, tel: 514 457-9371, 800 361-9371 (Québec), 800 465-9474 (US and Canada)
Tourisme Québec, 101 Ste-Catherine ouest, Montréal, tel: 514 873-7977 or toll-free 800-363-7777 from other parts of Canada and the US. Or check the province's website at: www.bonjour-quebec.com

The Outdoors

Details of fishing and hunting, licensing, can be obtained from Tourisme Québec, tel: 514 873-2015 or 800 363-7777.

Further information on the following sports can be obtained by telephoning the appropriate numbers below:
Camping, caravanning, tel: 514 252-3003
Canoeing, tel: 514 252-3001
Cross-country skiing, tel: 450 436-4051
Hang-gliding, tel: 514 856-4639
Hiking, tel: 514 252-3157
Horseback riding, tel: 514 252-3002
Mountain biking, tel: 514 252-3071

Rock climbing, tel: 514 252-3004
Sailing, tel: 514 252-3097
Scuba diving, tel: 514 252-3009
Snowmobiling, tel: 514 252-3076
Snowboarding, tel: 514 252 3089
Spelunking, tel: 514 252-3006

FURTHER READING

Stephen Scharper and Hilary Cunningham (eds), *Insight Guide: Montréal*, APA Publications, 1998. Insight Guides provide inspiring background information and are reliable on-the-spot companions.
Hilary Cunningham (ed), *Insight Guide: Canada*, APA Publications, 2000.
Alice Klement, *Insight Pocket Guide: Montréal*. APA Publications, 1998
Josh Freed, *Sign Language and Other Tales of Montréal Wildlife*, Montréal: Véhicle Press, 1990.
Mordecai Richler, *Oh, Canada! Oh, Québec! Requiem for a Divided Country*, Toronto: Penguin, 1992.
Aline Gubbay, *A Street Called the Main*, Montréal: Meridian, 1989.
Elaine Kalmna Nanes, *Writers of Montréal: Voix Parallèles/Parallel Voices*, Montréal: XYZ Editeur/Quarry, 1993
Barry Lazar and Tamsin Douglas, *Guide to Ethnic Montréal*, Montréal: Véhicule Press, 1993.
John Miesel, Guy Rochers and Arthur Silver, *As I recall/Si je me souviens bien*, Montréal: The Institute for Research on Public Policy, 1999.

Montréal mural

Index

ACKNOWLEDGMENTS

Photography Jonathan Wenk *and*

10, 12, 16T Archives Canada
2/3, 21B, 24, 27B, 30, 32, 33, 36, 40, Gera Dillon
41T&B, 42T&B, 49, 59T, 62T,
68, 69, 70B, 76, 77T, 88
26, 34, 37T&B, 39, 45T, 47B, Winston Fraser
48B, 54T, 57T, 58
63, 65T, 66, 67 Gouvernement de Québec
31B, 35B, 71, 83 Christian Guay
72T, 82T, 87 Alice Klement
38B McCord Museum of Canadian History
65B Ministre du Tourisme du Québec
14B Ontario Archives
52B Kathryn Presner
80 Carl Purcell
21T Pierre Soulard
64 Dominique Spriet/Wawati
15, 20, 23T&B, 25B, 29T&B, 52T, 55, Oscar Nelder
59B, 60T, 61, 70T, 73

Cover Photography Ed Simpson/Stone
Production Editor Mohammed Dar
Handwriting V Barl
Cartography Berndtson & Berndtson

NOTES

INSIGHT
Pocket Guides

Insight Pocket Guides pioneered a new
approach to guidebooks, introducing the
concept of the authors as "local hosts" who
would provide readers with personal
recommendations, just as they would give
honest advice to a friend who came to stay.
They also included a full-size pull-out map.

Now, to cope with the needs of the 21st
century, new editions in this growing series
are being given a new look to make them
more practical to use, and restaurant and
hotel listings have been greatly expanded.

Also from Insight Guides...

Insight Guides is the classic series, providing the complete picture with expert and informative text and stunning photography. Each book is an ideal travel planner, a reliable on-the-spot companion – and a superb visual souvenir of a trip. 193 titles.

Insight Maps are designed to complement the guidebooks. They provide full mapping of major destinations, and their laminated finish gives them ease of use and durability. 65 titles.

Insight Compact Guides are handy reference books, modestly priced yet comprehensive. The text, pictures and maps are all cross-referenced, making them ideal books to consult while seeing the sights. 119 titles.

INSIGHT POCKET GUIDE TITLES

Aegean Islands	California,	Israel	Moscow	Seville, Cordoba &
Algarve	Northern	Istanbul	Munich	Granada
Alsace	Canton	Jakarta	Nepal	Seychelles
Amsterdam	Chiang Mai	Jamaica	New Delhi	Sicily
Athens	Chicago	Kathmandu Bikes	New Orleans	Sikkim
Atlanta	Corsica	& Hikes	New York City	Singapore
Bahamas	Costa Blanca	Kenya	New Zealand	Southeast England
Baja Peninsula	Costa Brava	Kuala Lumpur	Oslo and	Southern Spain
Bali	Costa Rica	Lisbon	Bergen	Sri Lanka
Bali Bird Walks	Crete	Loire Valley	Paris	Sydney
Bangkok	Denmark	London	Penang	Tenerife
Barbados	Fiji Islands	Los Angeles	Perth	Thailand
Barcelona	Florence	Macau	Phuket	Tibet
Bavaria	Florida	Madrid	Prague	Toronto
Beijing	Florida Keys	Malacca	Provence	Tunisia
Berlin	French Riviera	Maldives	Puerto Rico	Turkish Coast
Bermuda	(Côte d'Azur)	Mallorca	Quebec	Tuscany
Bhutan	Gran Canaria	Malta	Rhodes	Venice
Boston	Hawaii	Manila	Rome	Vienna
Brisbane & the	Hong Kong	Marbella	Sabah	Vietnam
Gold Coast	Hungary	Melbourne	St. Petersburg	Yogjakarta
British Columbia	Ibiza	Mexico City	San Francisco	Yucatán Peninsula
Brittany	Ireland	Miami	Sarawak	
Brussels	Ireland's	Montreal	Sardinia	
Budapest	Southwest	Morocco	Scotland	